The City That Never Sleeps

The City That Never Sleeps

Poems of New York

Edited by

Shawkat M. Toorawa

Foreword by

Anne Pierson Wiese

excelsior editions

State University of New York Press
Albany, New York

Cover: Philip Lawrence Sherrod, "Eruption—42nd Street and 7th Avenue," © by Philip Sherrod 1977. Oil on canvas. Herbert F. Johnson Museum of Art, Cornell University, Permanent Collection.
Gift of Dr. Nathan Cohen. Used by permission of the artist.

Published by State University of New York Press, Albany

Printed in the United States of America

Excelsior Editions is an imprint of State University of New York Press

For information, contact State University of New York Press, Albany, NY
www.sunypress.edu

Production, Diane Ganeles
Marketing, Fran Keneston

Library of Congress Cataloging-in-Publication Data

The city that never sleeps : poems of New York / edited by Shawkat M. Toorawa ; foreword by Anne Pierson Wiese.
pages cm
Includes bibliographical references.
ISBN 978-1-4384-5615-7 (hardcover : alk. paper)
1. New York (N.Y.)—Poetry. 2. American poetry—20th century. 3. English poetry—20th century. 4. Poetry—Translations into English. 5. Poetry, Modern—20th century. I. Toorawa, Shawkat M., editor. II. Title: Poems of New York.
PN6110.P7N465 2015
808.81'93587471—dc23 2014021692

10 9 8 7 6 5 4 3 2 1

For my favorite visitors to New York—
Asiya, Maryam, and Parvine
and
for my favorite New Yorkers—
Marc and Michael,
and Ivonne

Even in the ironies, the allusiveness, the formal self-reference, the simultaneous evasion and acknowledgment of literary tradition that marks the poetry of the later twentieth century, there is something of the truly urban that transcends the merely urbane. And there is something to remind us that cities—each one configured differently—can seem to be figures for poetry itself.

—John Hollander

Contents

EVENING

NIGHT

Illustrations

Acknowledgments

One of the pleasures of putting together this anthology has been the opportunity to work with many individuals whom it is now also my pleasure to thank. I begin with fellow members of the short-lived 2NakedGuysCollective—Thalia Chrousos, Sophie Dosik, Erin Dougherty, Helen Havlak, Gabriela Jimenez, Kimberly Kent, Jackie Lam, Becca Litman, Andrew Lyon, Rabia Muqaddam, Meredith Shepard, Claire Snyder, Natalie Soto, Jerome Soustra, Ann Velazquez, and Tamer Yamani—who, as students in my spring 2010 poetry seminar, New York, Paris, Baghdad: Poetry of the City, provided for a semester of provocative discussion and helped produce an early incarnation of this anthology. Becca Litman and Rabia Muqaddam helped me source material and offered to copyedit.

Frank Robinson, Nancy Green, Cathy Klimaszewski, Liz Emrich, and Andrea Potochniak, at Cornell University's Herbert F. Johnson Museum of Art, gave me the opportunity to place twenty-four poems side-by-side with images in the exhibit New York, New York . . . It's a Hell of a Town. Former museum director Frank Robinson provided enthusiastic and early support of the idea of a published anthology, support graciously sustained by current museum director Stephanie Wiles. The museum generously provided the cover image and four interior images, selected in collaboration with Liz Emrich, who lent an expert eye; Samantha Gobioff assisted Liz in obtaining permissions.

Roger Gilbert, Gail Holst-Warhaft, Steve Maikowski, Jessica Papin, Peter Potter, Don Share, Lisa Russ Spaar, Alicia Stallings,

Christian Wiman, and Eric Zinner gave valuable early advice and encouragement.

The librarians and staff at Cornell's Olin Library provided invaluable assistance by making the BorrowDirect and Interlibrary loan process effortless. Peter Hirtle and Chip Rossetti on many occasions provided sage guidance about permissions.

The permissions directors, administrators, or literary executors I contacted were unfailingly helpful: Rosemary Bavister, Erica Bossier, Marie Brown, Anitra Budd, Katherine Chen, Emma Cheshire, Elizabeth Clementson, Jack Clinton, Sharla Clute, Frederick Courtright, Andrea Currie, Juanita DeSilva, Jenny Dorney, Suzanne Fairless-Aitken, Sherri Feldman, Kelsey Ford, Callie Gladman, Margaret Gorenstein, Ron Hussey, Dara Hyde, Bud Johns, Vie Kaufman, Diana Lachatanere, Babe Liberman, Denise Maurin, Kevin McGee, John McSpadyen, Ana Paz, Holly Peppe, David Pichaske, Claire Reinertsen, Susan Taylor Rash, Lauren Rogoff, Jennifer Rowley, Peter Salpeter, Harold Schmidt, Bianca Stone, Robert Sharrard, Samantha Shea, Erica Sheftic, and Craig Tenney. My special thanks to Peter London for his kind consideration; to Sherri Feldman for her kind indulgence; to William Kosmas, Esquire, and Christopher Maurer for allowing me to be part of Lorca's New York; and to Angie Hogan, for allowing me to be part of Senghor's New York, though, as always, I turned to Parvine Toorawa for advice and intuition about the French. Julie Graham handled the permissions payments effortlessly. Chrissy Capalongo, Shelly Marino, and Joshua Porter helped in many ways. Without the work of all of these good folk, this anthology could not have been.

Wayles Browne introduced me to the poetry of Sasha Skenderija and Stephanie Krueger; Robyn Creswell commented on a late version of the manuscript, which led to the inclusion of a passage from a Durs Grünbein poem, kindly sourced for me by Andreea Mascan. Fred Muratori's suggestion of John Brehm came too late in the process, but I am no less grateful to him.

Maryam Toorawa gave input on the Lorca translation, was an early advisor on selections and sequence, and helped me collate—

as did Asiya Toorawa. Maryam also helped with copyediting at every stage. Remaining shortcomings are of course mine.

Kim Haines-Eitzen, chair of the Department of Near Eastern Studies, colleague and friend, valued this work both for what it is and for what it meant to me from its very inception. So too: Stephanie Wiles, director of the Herbert F. Johnson Museum of Art, and Kent Fuchs, Cornell University Provost. I also received support from the following at Cornell, underscoring the value and appeal of poetry throughout the institution: Gerard Aching; Iftikhar Dadi, Department of Art; Laurent Ferri, French Studies Program; Dan Gold, South Asia Program; Mary Katzenstein, American Studies Program; Dean Kent Kleinman, College of Art, Architecture & Planning; Natalie Melas, Department of Comparative Literature; Tim Murray, Rose Goldsen Lecture Series of the College of Arts and Sciences; Steve Pond, Department of Music; Cynthia Robinson, Department of History of Art and Visual Studies; and Nic van de Walle, Department of Government. I cannot ever repay Ken McClane '69 or Vanessa Albert Lowry '85 for their generosity.

Lisa Russ Spaar's splendid anthology, *All That Mighty Heart: London Poems*, was the inspiration for the volume's shape; Anne Pierson Wiese's brilliant foreword contributes to the volume's feel. And the press's outside reader's astute comments were in many cases decisive. To all three, I am more grateful than they can know.

As for the many poets who gave me permission to include their work, the best way to express my gratitude is to say this: Your wonderful poetry is this book's and this labor (of love)'s *raison d'être*.

Parvine, Maryam, and Asiya have always shown endless and loving patience—and our cat, Cotomili, wondrous circumspection—for my obsessions. Thank you.

James Peltz at State University of New York Press has been an advocate and friend of this project since the very moment he learned about it. It has been a singular pleasure to work with him, Rafael Chaiken, Diane Ganeles, and Fran Keneston with the Press.

Copyright Acknowledgments

Adonis: "A Grave for New York," from *A Time Between Ashes and Roses*, translated by Shawkat M. Toorawa, copyright © 2004 by Syracuse University Press. Used by permission of Syracuse University Press.

Maya Angelou: "Awaking in New York," from *Shaker, Why Don't You Sing?* copyright © 1983 by Maya Angelou. Used by permission of Random House, Inc. Any third-party use of this material, outside of this publication, is prohibited. Interested parties must apply directly to Random House, Inc. for permission. Used also by permission of Virago, an imprint of Little Brown Book Group.

W. H. Auden: "September 1, 1939," from *W. H. Auden: The Collected Poems*, by W. H. Auden, copyright © 1940, renewed 1968. Used by permission of Random House, Inc. Any third-party use of this material, outside of this publication, is prohibited. Interested parties must apply directly to Random House, Inc. for permission. Used also by permission of Curtis Brown Ltd.

Gwendolyn Bennett: "Street Lamps in Early Spring," from *Opportunity: Journal of Negro Life* (May 1926), copyright © 1926 by the National Urban League. Used by permission of the National Urban League.

Ted Berrigan: "Sonnet XXXVI," from *The Sonnets*, by Ted Berrigan, copyright © 2000 by Alice Notley, Literary Executrix of the Estate of Ted Berrigan. Used by permission of Viking Penguin, a division of Penguin Group (USA) Inc.

Anna Hempstead Branch: "New York at Sunrise," from *The Shoes That Danced and Other Poems* (1905), by Anna Hempstead Branch.

Luis Cabalquinto: "August Walk," from *Mannahatta Mahal: Collected Expatriate Poems*, copyright © 2001, 2007 by Luis Cabalquinto. Used by permission of the author.

Alberto O. Cappas: "Maria's Journey," from *Doña Julia and Other Selected Poems*, copyright © 2002, 2009 by Alberto O. Cappas. Used by permission of the author.

Fay Chiang: "Snow," from *In the City of Contradictions*, copyright © 1979, 2010 by Fay Chiang. Used by permission of the author.

Robert Clairmont: "These Ever Just So Six Million New York Hearts and Dorothy," from *Quintillions* (1928), by Robert Clairmont.

Hart Crane: "To Brooklyn Bridge," from *Complete Poems of Hart Crane*, edited by Marc Simon, copyright © 1933, 1958, 1966 by Liveright Publishing Corporation, copyright © 1986 by Marc Simon. Used by permission of Liveright Publishing Corporation.

Victor Hernández Cruz: "The Lower East Side of Manhattan," from *Maraca: New and Selected Poems 1966–2000*, copyright © 1997 by Victor Hernández Cruz. Reprinted by permission of The Permissions Company, Inc., on behalf of Coffee House Press, www.coffeehousepress.org.

E. E. Cummings: "at the ferocious phenomenon of 5 o'clock," copyright ©1925, 1953, 1991 by the Trustees for the E. E. Cummings Trust, copyright © 1976 by George James Firmage, from *Complete Poems: 1904–1962*, by E. E. Cummings, edited by George J. Firmage. Used by permission of Liveright Publishing Corporation.

Mahmoud Darwish: From "As Fate Would Have It," from *Unfortunately, It Was Paradise*, translated by Munir Akash and Carolyn Forché, copyright © 2003, 2013 by University of California Press. Used by permission of The Regents of the University of California.

Bob Dylan: "Desolation Row." Words and music by Bob Dylan. Copyright © 1965 by Warner Bros. Inc; renewed 1993 by Special Rider Music. All Rights Reserved. Reprinted by permission.

Shokry Eldaly: "I Had This Dream/the city of shadows," copyright © 2013 by Shokry Eldaly. Used by permission of the author.

Martín Espada: "The Mexican Cabdriver's Poem for His Wife, Who Has Left Him," from *A Mayan Astronomer in Hell's Kitchen*, by Martín Espada, copyright © 2000 by Martín Espada. Used by permission of the author and W. W. Norton & Company, Inc.

Allen Ginsberg: "Mugging," from *Collected Poems, 1947–1980*, by Allen Ginsberg. Copyright © 1984 by Allen Ginsberg. Reprinted by permission of HarperCollins Publishers.

Nikki Giovanni: "The New Yorkers," from *Cotton Candy on a Rainy Day*, by Nikki Giovanni, copyright © 1978 by Nikki Giovanni. Reprinted by permission of HarperCollins Publishers.

Durs Grünbein: "Peacocks on Broadway," from *The Palm Beach Effect*, edited by André Naffis-Sahély and Julian Stannard, translated by Andrew Shields, copyright © 2012, 2013 by Durs Grünbein and Andrew Shields. Used by permission of Andrew Shields.

Jessica Hagedorn: "Latin Music in New York," from *Danger and Beauty*, by Jessica Hagedorn, copyright © 2002 by Jessica Hagedorn. Reprinted by permission of City Lights Books.

John Hollander: "New York," from *Spectral Emanations: New and Selected Poems*, by John Hollander, copyright © 1978 John Hollander. Used by permission of the author.

Langston Hughes: "Juke Box Love Song," from *The Collected Poems of Langston Hughes*, by Langston Hughes, edited by Arnold Rampersad with David Roessel, associate editor, copyright © 1994 by the Estate of Langston Hughes. Used by permission of Alfred A. Knopf, a division of Random House, Inc. Any third-party use of this material, outside of this publication, is prohibited. Interested parties must apply directly to Random House, Inc. for permission. Additional rights by permission of Harold Ober Associates Incorporated.

Donald Justice: "Manhattan Dawn (1945)," from *Collected Poems*, by Donald Justice, copyright © 2004 by Donald Justice. Used by permission of Alfred A. Knopf, a division of Random House, Inc. Any third-party use of this material, outside of this publication, is prohibited. Interested parties must apply directly to Random House, Inc. for permission.

Galway Kinnell: "The Avenue Bearing the Initial of Christ into the New World." From *What a Kingdom It Was: Poems*, by Galway Kinnell copyright © 1960, renewed 1988 by Galway Kinnell. Reprinted by permission of Houghton Mifflin Company. All rights reserved.

Stephanie Krueger: "Cyclone," from *Spirit of Bosnia*, vol. 7, no. 1, copyright © 2012 by Stephanie Krueger. Used by permission of the author.

Denise Levertov: "February Evening in New York," by Denise Levertov, from *Collected Early Poems, 1940–1960*, copyright © 1960 by Denise Levertov. Reprinted by permission of New Directions Publishing Corp.

Vachel Lindsay: "A Rhyme About an Electrical Sign," from *The Poetry of Vachel Lindsay*, edited by Dennis Camp, 3 vols., Peoria, Illinois: Spoon River Poetry Press, 1984, 1985, 1986, copyright © 1986 by Spoon River Press. Reprinted by permission of Spoon River Press.

Federico García Lorca: "New York (Office and Denunciation)," by Federico García Lorca, copyright © Federico García Lorca. Translation by Shawkat M. Toorawa, copyright © 2013 by Shawkat M. Toorawa and Herederos de Federico García Lorca. Used by permission.

Amy Lowell: "New York at Night," from *The Complete Poetical Works of Amy Lowell*, copyright © 1955 by Houghton Mifflin Company, copyright renewed 1983 by Houghton Mifflin Company, Brinton P. Roberts, and G. D'Andelot Belin, Esquire. Reprinted by permission of Houghton Mifflin Harcourt Publishing Company. All rights reserved.

Robert Lowell: "Central Park," from *Collected Poems by Robert Lowell*, copyright © 2003 by Harriet Lowell and Sheridan Lowell. Reprinted by permission of Farrar, Straus and Giroux, L.L.C.

Anna Margolin: "Evening on Fifth Avenue," from *Drunk from the Bitter Truth: The Poems of Anna Margolin*, by Anna Margolin, translated by Shirley Kumove, copyright © 2005 by State University of New York Press. Reprinted by permission of State University of New York Press.

Kenneth McClane: "Sunday Morning," from *To Hear the River*, by Kenneth McClane, copyright © 1981 by Kenneth McClane. Reprinted by permission of the author.

Claude McKay: "Dawn in New York," from *Selected Poems of Claude McKay*, copyright © 1953 by Bookman Associates, renewed 1981 by Twayne Publishers. Reprinted courtesy of the Literary Representative for the Works of Claude McKay, Schomburg Center for Research in Black Culture, The New York Public Library, Astor, Lenox and Tilden Foundations.

Edna St. Vincent Millay: "MacDougal Street," from *A Few Figs from Thistles* (1922), by Edna St. Vincent Millay.

Valzhyna Mort: "New York," from *Poetry* (April 2009). Copyright © 2009 by Valzhyna Mort. Used by permission of the author.

Frank O'Hara: "A Step Away from Them," by Frank O'Hara, from *Lunch Poems*, copyright ©1964 by Frank O'Hara. Reprinted by permission of City Lights Books.

Sharon Olds: "Summer Solstice, New York City," from *The Gold Cell*, by Sharon Olds, copyright © 1987 by Sharon Olds. Used by permission of Alfred A. Knopf, a division of Random House, Inc. Any third-party use of this material, outside of this publication, is prohibited. Interested parties must apply directly to Random House, Inc., for permission.

Nicanor Parra: "Resurrección," ANTIPOEMAS, copyright © Nicanor Parra, 1960. "Resurrection," from *Antipoems: New and Selected*, translated by Liz Werner, copyright © 1985 by Nicanor Parra. Reprinted by permission of New Directions Publishing Corp. Additional rights by permission of Agencia Literaria Carmen Balcells.

Willie Perdomo: "123rd Street Rap," from *Where a Nickel Costs a Dime*, by Willie Perdomo, copyright © 1996 by Willie Perdomo. Used by permission of W. W. Norton & Company, Inc. Additional rights by permission of Marie Brown Associates.

Melanie Rehak: "Autobiography: New York," from *The New Yorker* (October 16, 2006), copyright © 2006 by Melanie Rehak. Used by permission of the author.

Adrienne Rich: Poems XVI and XX from *Twenty-One Love Poems*, copyright © 2013 by The Adrienne Rich Literary Trust, copyright © 1978 by W. W. Norton & Company, Inc. from *Later Poems: Selected and New, 1971–2012*, by Adrienne Rich. Used by permission of W. W. Norton & Company, Inc.

Edwin Rolfe: "Season of Death," from *Collected Poems*, by Edwin Rolfe, edited by Cary Nelson and Jefferson Hendricks, copyright 1993 © by the Board of Trustees of the University of Illinois. Used by permission of the editors and the University of Illinois Press.

Carl Sandburg: "Broadway," from *The Complete Poems of Carl Sandburg*, copyright © 1970, 1969 by Lilian Steichen Sandburg, Trustee. Reprinted by permission of the Carl Sandburg Family Trust and Houghton Mifflin Harcourt, Inc.

James Schuyler: "The Morning," from *Collected Poems*, by James Schuyler, copyright © 1993 by the Estate of James Schuyler. Reprinted by permission of Farrar, Straus and Giroux, L.L.C.

David Semanki: "Rain," from *Poems of New York*, edited by Elizabeth Schmidt, copyright © 2002 by David Semanki. Reprinted by permission of the author.

Léopold Sédar Senghor: "To New York," from *Éthiopiques*, by Léopold Sédar Senghor. Translation by Shawkat M. Toorawa, copyright © 2013 by Shawkat M. Toorawa, and printed by permission of the University of Virginia Press.

Purvi Shah: "Made in India: Immigrant Song #3," from *Terrain Tracks*, by Purvi Shah, copyright © 2006 by Purvi Shah. Reprinted by permission of the author.

Meredith Shepard: "Why I Hate New York," by Meredith Shepard, copyright © 2011. Used by permission of the author.

Charles Simic: "Early Morning in July," from *Hotel Insomnia*, by Charles Simic, copyright © 1992 by Charles Simic. Reprinted by permission of Houghton Mifflin Company. All rights reserved.

Paul Simon: "The 59th Street Bridge Song (Feelin' Groovy)." Words and music by Paul Simon. Copyright ©1996, 1967 Paul Simon (BMI). International copyright secured. All rights reserved. Used by permission. Warning: Unauthorized reproduction of this publication is prohibited by Federal Law and is subject to criminal prosecution.

Sasha Skenderija: "West Side Story," from *Cape of Good Hope: Poems*, by Sasha Skenderija, translated by Wayles Browne, copyright © 2011 by Sasha Skenderija. Reprinted by permission of the author.

Tom Sleigh: "New York American Spell, 2001," from *Far Side of the Earth: Poems*, by Tom Sleigh, copyright © 2003 by Tom Sleigh. Reprinted by permission of Houghton Mifflin Company. All rights reserved.

Herman Spector: "Wiseguy Type," from *Bastard in the Ragged Suit*, edited by Bud Johns and Judith Clancy, copyright © 1977 by Synergistic Press. Used by permission of Synergistic Press.

Sara Teasdale: "From the Woolworth Tower," from *Rivers to the Sea* (1915), by Sara Teasdale.

Tomas Tranströmer: "Schubertiana," from *New Collected Poems*, translated by Robin Fulton, copyright © 1987, 1997, 2002, 2006 by Tomas Tranströmer, translation copyright © 1987, 1997, 2002, 2006 by Robin Fulton. Reprinted by permission of Bloodaxe Books.

Derek Walcott: "God Rest Ye Merry, Gentlemen," from *Collected Poems, 1948–1984*, by Derek Walcott, copyright © 1986 by Derek Walcott. Reprinted by permission of Farrar, Straus and Giroux, L.L.C. Additional rights by permission of Faber & Company.

Anne Pierson Wiese: "Body Elite," from *Floating City*, by Anne Pierson Wiese, copyright © 2007. Reprinted by permission of Louisiana State University Press.

Walt Whitman: "When I Heard at the Close of Day," from *Leaves of Grass* (1860, 1867), by Walt Whitman.

Nathaniel Parker Willis: "City Lyrics," from *The Poems, Sacred, Passionate and Humorous of Nathaniel Parker Willis* (1844), by Nathaniel Parker Willis.

Franz Wright: "Arriving in the City," from *Earlier Poems*, by Franz Wright, copyright © 2007 by Franz Wright. Used by permission of Alfred A. Knopf, a division of Random House, Inc. Any third-party use of this material, outside of this publication, is prohibited. Interested parties must apply directly to Random House, Inc. for permission.

Every effort was made to contact all copyright holders. Any unacknowledged copyright holders are asked to contact State University of New York Press.

Publication of this work was made possible by support from Vanessa Albert Lowry, Cornell '85; Kenneth McClane, Cornell '69; and by support of the following at Cornell University: Department of Near Eastern Studies; Herbert F. Johnson Museum of Art; Office of the Provost; American Studies Program; Department of Art; Department of Comparative Literature; Department of the History of Art and Visual Studies; Department of Government; Department of Music; French Studies Program; Office of the Dean, College of Art, Architecture and Planning; Rose Goldsen Lecture Series of the College of Arts and Sciences; South Asia Program; and by support from The Research Foundation for the State University of New York.

Foreword

"My eye," my great-aunt, Tante Ruby, used to say. It was, coming from her, an expression of mild wonderment, meant as encouragement to continue with whatever story one was telling. She said it the same way that other women of her generation said, "My stars!"

Tante Ruby, the wife of a Minnesota farmer whom she outlived by three decades, came to visit my family only once when I was growing up in Brooklyn. In those days there was still some thought of dressing up for airplane travel, and I remember that when she got off the plane at LaGuardia Airport her jacket matched her dress, her handbag matched her shoes, and she was wearing a big brooch shaped like a daisy. One night, we ordered take-out Chinese food to give her a real New York experience. Tante Ruby, gamely navigating her first-ever plastic packet of soy sauce, wound up squirting herself in the eye. We never forgot.

Many years later—decades later—when I flew from New York wearing jeans and a sweatshirt to visit Tante Ruby in Minnesota, she was over ninety years old and her eyesight had failed. Her wits were as sharp as could be, though, and she still lived in her own small house in town, which she kept neat as a pin despite being legally blind. We sat in her company room—spotless, with everything in it at right angles to everything else—and she gestured toward the open windows that faced out onto her front yard and Dodge Street, a vista that for her must have been an extensive blur dappled with the green light that filtered through the grand old trees lining the block and disturbed by the occasional fin-and-ripple motion of a passing car. "Some folks like to keep their curtains closed," she said. "I suppose they're worried about people looking in. But what I say is, you got to look out while you can look out."

To be a waitress in New York City you have to walk on windows. I am thinking in particular of a recent evening on which, having received my annual $30 Benihana Birthday Gift Certificate, I went with my husband for our once-a-year hibachi dinner at Benihana's on 56th Street in Manhattan. We sat with our backs almost touching the floor-to-ceiling glass window overlooking 56th Street, at one of the many horseshoe-shaped counters designed to accommodate eight diners. In the center the chef, with his tall paper hat, his belt of knives, and sleight-of-hand skills to equal any magician, sliced, diced, and meticulously produced our eight different meals on an expanse of grill that was red hot in the center with descending levels of heat toward its edges, allowing him to cook different ingredients at different temperatures. Every year we wait with anticipatory glee for the onion-slice-volcano trick, the beautiful spinning egg, the shrimp-in-hat act, and every year a different chef performs these maneuvers flawlessly. Meanwhile, in order to deliver soup, salad, and beverages to those of us wedged in with our backs to 56th Street, the waitress edged behind us with balletic grace along the six-inch-wide bottom of the window—walking on what is technically known as a windowsill.

"It's a poem," I said.

"Write it down," said my husband.

"I don't have any paper," I admitted as reluctantly as might a doctor caught without her stethoscope, facing a patient in the emergency room.

My husband silently handed me his paper napkin, only slightly soiled, and his felt-tip pen. The word *window* grew blurry green edges as I inscribed it on the napkin. In the dimness I squinted to see what I was writing.

New York, the city that never sleeps, contains more light than all the myriad heavens conceived of by its denizens of every possible race, religion, culture, color, and creed combined. All poets are besotted with light: It is the most transformative of all phenomena and we are permanently drunk on it—moon mad, sun blind, star struck.

Wherever you look in New York City there is light: Peering through the metal grates of the street sewers you glimpse needles of sky reflected in the wet, unseemly murk below; the sun shines so brightly one spring day as you walk through a neighborhood park in Brooklyn it takes a while to realize that what you have paused to admire is not just light caught and released into a pool at ground level by an infinity of heart-shaped leaves but a field of tiny white violets—flowers and light indistinguishable; at sunrise or sunset, if you stare down the streets in Manhattan that run east-west across the width of the island, you see a tunnel of river-refracted light, a tunnel lined with windows that catch that light and turn fleetingly into flocks of white birds; at night in New York, everything emits light: the swerving halogen gaze of each moving vehicle, the craning alien globes of the street lamps, the silent film flickering in every storefront, the half-lit skyscrapers looking like control panels for some enormous, obscure endeavor, and the lights in the houses and apartment buildings where people live—smaller and more explicable.

New York City is the place from which you famously cannot see the stars in the sky for all the interposing lights of our own human creations; it is also the place where, as Vachel Lindsay imagined, "The signs in the streets and the signs in the skies/Shall make a new Zodiac, guiding the wise. . . ." My eye.

—Anne Pierson Wiese
New York City, May 2013

Preface

On Wednesday mornings in the spring of 2010, I taught a seminar titled New York, Paris, Baghdad: Poetry of the City. Before class, we would meet in the Two Naked Guys Café at Cornell's Johnson Museum of Art, where Kathy Straight cheerfully plied us with coffee, tea, and pastries as we began our conversations about that week's poet and city. We discussed Adonis, Baudelaire, Cavafy, Lorca, Whitman, and many others to discover how these poets have read the city, how they have written it, and how other poets have responded.

One week, we hatched the idea of producing a class anthology of New York poetry—based on our readings and our sensibilities. Each of us selected four or five pieces for possible inclusion, and on two subsequently animated Wednesdays we refined our corpus to fifty-four poems. A conversation with then-director of the Johnson Museum, Frank Robinson, led to the idea of exhibiting some of those poems together with pieces from the museum's collections. Guided by curator Nancy Green, and with input from the students, I selected poems and artwork. Thus was born the exhibit New York, New York . . . It's a Hell of a Town, featuring twenty-four poems and twenty-four pieces of art.[1] The aim was to have the juxtapositions give readers and visitors new ways of thinking about both the words and the images.

The poetry and artwork were not distributed around the exhibit chronologically or alphabetically but aesthetically—in ways that allowed the poems and paintings and photographs to interact in the space. The exhibit gave me the idea of producing an anthology proper, notably one in which poems might similarly interact. While pondering how to accomplish this, I came upon Lisa Russ Spaar's wonderful collection, *All That Mighty Heart: London Poems*, which she organizes according to the four elements: Water, Earth, Fire, and Air. I reread the poems from the exhibit to see if there was a principle I could similarly apply, and I noticed that many, if not most, poems could be situated at specific points in a New York day: dawn (McKay), 5 o'clock (Cummings), evening (Wiese), night (Rich), midnight (Dylan), and so on. This is how I settled on Morning, Day, Evening, and Night.

In choosing material, I let myself be guided neither by the need to be representative (whatever that might in fact mean) nor by the need to be inclusive—there are already many comprehensive collections (see the list of further reading at the end of the volume). Nevertheless, like the exhibit, this anthology tries to range widely—and I hope deeply—and yet the goal has not been to seek out individual poets or specific poems. It is true that at times a particular poem seemed to want to find a way in, but I would decide it did not quite belong; at other times I wanted to include a personal favorite, but I resisted. Although I set almost every such poem aside, I did keep two: Valzyhna Mort's magical "New York," which I have placed at the beginning as an invitation into the collection and into New York; and Robert Clairmont's plaintive "These Ever Just So Six Million Hearts and Dorothy," which I have placed at the end as an envoi and as an invitation to return—both to the city and to the anthology. Ultimately, I did not choose poems because they fit one of the four rubrics, but because they were, to my mind, good poems, strong poems.

Many canonical New York poets are not represented in these pages, figures such as John Ashbery or David Lehman, but other avowedly New York poets missed by other anthologies are here: Luis Cabalquinto, Jessica Hagedorn, and Anna Margolin, for example. I also paid special attention to up-and-coming voices, such as Shokry Eldaly and Purvi Shah. The lyrics of New Yorker

Paul Simon and of Bob Dylan also find a natural place in this collection. I also thought it essential to include New York poems by world poets, such as Mahmoud Darwish and Nicanor Parra, Derek Walcott and Tomas Tranströmer. This orchestra of local, immigrant, and foreign voices is, it seems to me, apposite and fitting.

A small measure of the new ground this collection breaks, then, is that of the 149 poems (or extracts) in its most immediate predecessor, Stephen Wolf's *I Speak of the City: Poems of New York* (2007), only twenty appear here.[2] Of the 128 poems in the other major recent collection, Elizabeth Schmidt's *Poems of New York* (2002), only five appear here.[3] When it comes to poets, the numbers are admittedly higher: thirty-one out of the 138 poets in Wolf's anthology are included, as are twenty-three out of the eighty-four poets in Schmidt's. This higher degree of poet overlap is not surprising, as those who have sung New York have done so in ways that are hard to ignore. Song is partly why I chose a phrase from Sinatra's (properly, Kander and Ebb's) "New York, New York" as the collection's title—*The City That Never Sleeps*. But a more important reason is the fact that a great number of poets long to be awake while everyone else is asleep and are inspired by the New York night and its early morning light.[4] Senghor calls out, "Nights of insomnia, O Nights of Manhattan!"

Stephen Wolf and Elizabeth Schmidt will I trust forgive me for saying that their earlier collections are nostalgic, reverential, even patriotic.[5] Wolf says of his anthology,

> All the poems in this book speak of New York, and many poems are intrinsically American as well. . . . New York remains a symbol to the world of both this nation and the modern cosmopolis. . . . *I Speak of the City* is a testament to the city's spirit, preserved and newly created in the most ennobling expression of the human heart.[6]

Schmidt writes of hers,

> The poems collected in this anthology . . . all share a desire to record the fleeting, shifting, "parti-colored" essences of New York life in their own particular form and diction. . . . Poets who have written about New York are masters at preserving, and allowing us to cherish, moments of life in this theater of chance and change.[7]

To be sure, *The City That Never Sleeps* tries to capture New York City in its many moods and expressions—but it also tries to avoid being adulatory. Besides giving the reader the opportunity to experience twenty-four hours in New York through poetry, it tries to put poems and poets in new conversation with each other, in debate, even on occasion in conflict. And it attempts to illustrate some of the ways in which poetry has given imaginative reality to the city, just as much as urban changes have in turn transformed the poetic text.[8]

Not every poet loves New York, but each and every one is mesmerized by it. Maybe it is because, as John Hollander has put it, "there is something to remind us that cities—each one configured differently—can seem to be figures for poetry itself."[9] There is evidently also something about *poems*—each one configuring differently—that seems to make them figures for the city. E. B. White recognized this sixty-five years ago in *Here Is New York* (1949): "The city is like poetry: it compresses all life, all races and breeds, into a small island and adds music and the accompaniment of internal engines."[10] When I first visited New York some twenty years after White wrote those lines, I was only four, but my most vivid memories are in fact of vibrant sounds—horns, engines, shouts, sirens, laughter, music . . . Paris, where I lived at the time, and London before that, were not as loud or brash or lively; Hong Kong, Singapore, Philadelphia, Cairo, Delhi, where I lived after, simply did not—do not—quite have what Lisa Russ

Spaar has described as New York's "operatic bravado."[11] It is my earnest hope that *The City That Never Sleeps* captures some of that, some of the city's tumult, its arias, its rhythms.

—Shawkat M. Toorawa
Ithaca, NY, January 2014

Notes

1. See http: //cornellsun.com/node/46845 (accessed 12 January 2014).

2. *I Speak of the City: Poems of New York*, selected and edited by Stephen Wolf (New York: Columbia University Press, 2007).

3. *Poems of New York*, selected and edited by Elizabeth Schmidt (New York and Toronto: Alfred A. Knopf, 2002).

4. I am grateful to the press's outside reader for pointing this out. See, in this connection, *Acquainted with the Night: Insomnia Poems*, edited by Lisa Russ Spaar (New York: Columbia University Press, 1999).

5. See *Poems of New York*, ed. Schmidt, 19, and *I Speak of the City: Poems of New York*, ed. Wolf, xxx, respectively, for further characterizations of the editors' motivations in producing their anthologies.

6. *I Speak of the City: Poems of New York*, ed. Wolf, xxx, xxxi.

7. *Poems of New York*, ed. Schmidt, 18–19, 20.

8. To paraphrase Richard Lehan, *The City in Literature: An Intellectual and Cultural History* (Berkeley: University of California Press, 1998), xv.

9. John Hollander, Foreword, in *I Speak of the City: Poems of New York*, ed. Wolf, xv.

10. E. B. White, *Here Is New York* (New York: Harper, 1949), 29.

11. *All That Mighty Heart: London Poems*, edited by Lisa Russ Spaar (Charlottesville and London: University of Virginia Press, 2008), 6.

Valzhyna Mort

New York

new york, madame,
                    is a monument to a city

it is
TA-DA
a gigantic pike
whose scales
bristled up stunned

and what used to be just smoke
found a fire that gave it birth

champagne foam
melted into metal
glass rivers
flowing upwards
and things you won't tell to a priest
you reveal to a cabdriver

even time is sold out
when to the public's "wow" and "shhh"
out of a black top hat
a tailed magician
is pulling new york out
by the ears of skyscrapers

—Translated from the Belarusian by Franz Wright and Elizabeth Oehlkers Wright

Marilyn Bridges, "Chrysler Building, New York City 1988," © Marilyn Bridges 1988. Gelatin silver print. Used by permission of the photographer.

Morning

MAYA ANGELOU

Awaking in New York

Curtains forcing their will
against the wind,
children sleep,
exchanging dreams with
seraphim. The city
drags itself awake on
subway straps; and
I, an alarm, awake as a
rumor of war,
lie stretching into dawn,
unasked and unheeded.

Claude McKay

Dawn in New York

The Dawn! The Dawn! The crimson-tinted, comes
Out of the low still skies, over the hills,
Manhattan's roofs and spires and cheerless domes!
The Dawn! My spirit to its spirit thrills.
Almost the mighty city is asleep,
No pushing crowd, no tramping, tramping feet.
But here and there a few cars groaning creep
Along, above, and underneath the street,
Bearing their strangely-ghostly burdens by,
The women and the men of garish nights,
Their eyes wine-weakened and their clothes awry,
Grotesques beneath the strong electric lights.
The shadows wane. The Dawn comes to New York.
And I go darkly-rebel to my work.

Anna Hempstead Branch

New York at Sunrise

When with her clouds the early dawn illumes
Our doubtful streets, wistful they grow and mild;
As if a sleeping soul grew happy and smiled,
The whole dark city radiantly blooms.
Pale spires lift their hands above the glooms
Like a resurrection, delicately wild,
And flushed with slumber like a little child,
Under a mist, shines forth the innocent Tombs.
Thus have I seen it from a casement high.
As unsubstantial as a dream it grows.
Is this Manhattan, virginal and shy,
That in a cloud so rapturously glows?
Ethereal, frail, and like an opening rose,
I see my city with an enlightened eye.

Donald Justice

Manhattan Dawn (1945)

There is a smoke of memory
That curls about these chimneys
And then uncurls; that lifts,
Diaphanous, from sleep

To lead us down some alleyway
Still vaguely riverward;
And so at length disperses
Into the wisps and tatters

That garland fire escapes.
—And we have found ourselves again
Watching, beside a misty platform,
The first trucks idling to unload

(New England's frost still
Unstippling down their sides).
                                        Or turned
To catch blue truant eyes upon us

Through steam that rose up suddenly from a grate . . .
                                        Grinning—
And the grin slid off across the storefronts.
Dawn always seemed to overtake us, though,

Down Hudson somewhere, or Horatio.
—And we have seen it bend
The long stripes of the awnings down
Toward gutters where discarded flowers

Lay washing in the night's small rain—
Hints, glimmerings of a world
Not ours.
                    And office towers
Coast among lost stars.

Adonis ('Ali Ahmad Sa'id) ~

From "A Grave for New York"

I

Until now, the Earth has been depicted in the shape of a pear
by which I mean a breast
Yet, the difference between breast and tomb is a mere technicality:
New York
A four-legged civilization; in every direction is murder or a road to murder
and in the distance are the moans of the drowned.

New York,
A woman—the statue of a woman
in one hand she holds a scrap to which the documents we call history give the name "liberty," and in the other she smothers a child whose name is Earth.

New York,
A body the color of asphalt. Around her waist is a damp girdle, her face is a closed window . . . I said: Walt Whitman will open it—"I speak the password primeval"—but no one hears it except an unreturning god. The prisoners, the slaves, the despairing, the thieves, the diseased spew from his throat. There is no outlet, no path. And I said: "The Brooklyn Bridge!" But it's the bridge that connects Whitman to Wall Street, that connects leaves-grass to paper-dollars . . .

New York–Harlem,
Who comes in a guillotine of silk, who leaves in a grave the length of the Hudson? Explode, you ritual of tears. Cling together, you trifles of exhaustion. Blue, yellow, roses, jasmine: the light sharpens its points, and in the pinprick the sun is

born. Have you ignited, O wound, concealed between thigh and thigh? Has the bird of death come to you and have you heard the death rattle? A rope, and the neck weaving melancholy; and in the blood, the melancholy of the Hour . . .

—*Translated from the Arabic by Shawkat M. Toorawa*

Federico García Lorca

New York (Office and Denunciation)

To Fernando Vela

Beneath the multiplications
is a drop of duck's blood.
Beneath the divisions
is a drop of sailor's blood.
Beneath the additions, a river of tender blood,
a wending river that sings
past the suburban bedrooms;
it is silver or concrete or wind
in the false dawn of New York.
Mountains exist, I know.
And eyeglasses for wisdom,
I know. But I have not come to see the sky.
I have come to see murky blood,
blood that carries the machines to the cataracts
and the spirit to the cobra's tongue.
In New York, every day,
four million ducks,
five million pigs,
two thousand pigeons, are killed to please the dying,
one million cows,
one million lambs,
two million roosters,
leave the sky in tatters.
Better to sob, as you sharpen the blade
or to murder dogs on raving hunts,
than to resist in early morning
those interminable convoys of milk,
those interminable convoys of blood,
those convoys of roses handcuffed

by the perfume sellers.
The ducks and pigeons,
the pigs and lambs,
lay their drops of blood
under the multiplications,
the horrific shrieks of cows wrung dry,
fill the valley with pain
where the Hudson becomes drunk with oil.

I denounce all
who ignore the other half,
the irredeemable half,
who raise their mountains of cement
where the hearts
of small forgotten animals beat
and where all of us will fall
in the final feast of power drills.

I spit in your faces.
The other half are listening,
devouring, singing, making off in their purity
like the children of superintendants
carrying tiny brittle sticks
to hollows where insect
antennae are rusting away.
This isn't hell, it's the street.
This isn't death, it's the fruit stand.
There is a world of broken rivers and distances out of reach
in the small paw of a cat, shattered by a motorcar,
and I hear the earthworm's song
in the hearts of countless young girls.
Rust, ferment, trembling earth.
You yourself are earth, swimming in office numbers.
What do I do? Rearrange the landscape?
Rearrange loves that will soon just be photographs,

that will soon just be pieces of wood and swigs of blood?
No, no; I denounce—
I denounce the connivance
of these deserted offices
that will not broadcast the suffering,
that stamp out the forest's plans
and I offer myself as a meal for cows wrung dry
when their cries fill the valley
where the Hudson becomes drunk with oil.

—*Translated from the Spanish by Shawkat M. Toorawa*

James Schuyler

The morning

breaks in splendor on
the window glass of
the French doors to
the shallow balcony
of my room with a
cast-iron balustrade
in a design of flowers,
mechanical and coarse
and painted black:
sunbursts of a coolish
morning in July. I
almost accept the fact
that I am not in
the country, where I
long to be, but in
this place of glass
and stone—and metal,
let's not forget
metal—where traffic sounds and the day
is well begun. So
be it, morning.

Charles Simic

Early Morning in July

The streets were cool
After the heat of the night.
The dives, their doors open,
Smelled of stale beer.
Someone swept the floor
With even strokes.
He was pale as Confucius.
Martha Washington, her hair in a beehive,
Yawned in the glass booth
Of a movie theater.

Yesterday I saw Ulysses
Make Greek pastry.
Joan of Arc was at the dry cleaner's
Standing on a chair
With pins in her mouth.
St. Francis sold piranhas in a pet store.
At midnight Circe's daughters
Flew on a motorcycle.
Thomas Alva Edison
Roamed the streets in white socks
And blood on his shirt.

And now this sea breeze,
This unexpected coolness.
The small, sickly tree on your block
Hasn't grown much in years.
It shivers with happiness
With its few remaining leaves,
As if Emanuel Swedenborg
Was now whispering to the spirits
On Eighth Avenue.

Kenneth McClane

Sunday Morning

At the center it all doesn't
matter: I've said it before. I've
tried all those things which promise to save
us, I mean, I've waded through the tennis

motionings, have roosted in
the pale ambiences (glass always warm
in hand), have
crisscrossed my family, darkened every
hatching of life, blotched even the sour
last thought of a prisoner. Nothing:

Nothing has given anything back.
I was thinking it is sad
that we see the world in language: we don't
really know the wind, the thornberry, the raccoon

who so easily slips from country
to city: who grows fat in the sewers: who
realizes that a life is a life.

And I would walk along the Hudson,
see the condoms swelling
like ghosts, envision some aspect best not
included, reasoned with. I don't like

myself. I don't trust
a voice which so glibly
flashes in the morning, titillating in the absolute
denial of what is.

This is not pretty. It is a building
which stops short of its architect, a child
who finds his only need is air
and that breath fails.

Sasha Skenderija

West Side Story

A girl hurriedly crosses the street:
a Starbucks coffee in one hand,
pressing a phone to her ear with the other.

I try to develop the scene
to add some twist to the plot,
anything—
a traffic accident,
a puff on a cigarette,
melancholy.

In vain.

—Translated from the Bosnian by Wayles Browne

Stephanie Krueger

Cyclone

a child in rubber boots
wonders in the underground
at the dripping grates
holds up his hand to catch an emulsion
of machine oil and water
tells the rush hour crowd
how he captured the sky
there's endless worrying about the simple fact
about a stormy season
the weather reports indicate showers
at more than half probability
and the shoulders in the underground deflate
umbrella sellers reach with extended hand
offering prayers in silence
to those in mourning
the pre-written obituary database
hasn't been completely finished
MJ is dead
and from the second stories
records dusted off start turning
aimed at passersby
there's the white space
yet to be filled up

Ted Berrigan ~

Sonnet XXXVI

after Frank O'Hara

It's 8:54 a.m. in Brooklyn it's the 28th of July and
it's probably 8:54 in Manhattan but I'm
in Brooklyn I'm eating English muffins and drinking
pepsi and I'm thinking of how Brooklyn is New
York city too how odd I usually think of it as
something all its own like Bellows Falls like Little
Chute like Uijongbu
                                        I never thought on the Williams-
burg bridge I'd come so much to Brooklyn
just to see lawyers and cops who don't even carry
guns taking my wife away and bringing her back
                                                                                No
and I never thought Dick would be back at Gude's
beard shaved off long hair cut and Carol reading
his books when we were playing cribbage and
watching the sun come up over the Navy Yard
across the river
                                    I think I was thinking when I was
ahead I'd be somewhere like Perry street erudite
dazzling slim and badly loved
contemplating my new book of poems
to be printed in simple type on old brown paper
feminine marvelous and tough

Paul Simon

The 59th Street Bridge Song (Feelin' Groovy)

Slow down, you move too fast
You got to make the morning last
Just kicking down the cobblestones
Looking for fun and feelin' groovy
Ba da da da da da da, feelin' groovy

Hello, lamppost, what'cha knowin'?
I've come to watch your flowers growin'
Ain't'cha got no rhymes for me?
Doot-in doo-doo, feelin' groovy
Ba da da da da da da, feelin' groovy

I got no deeds to do
No promises to keep
I'm dappled and drowsy and ready to sleep
Let the morning time drop all its petals on me
Life, I love you
All is groovy

VICTOR HERNÁNDEZ CRUZ

The Lower East Side of Manhattan

By the East River
of Manhattan Island
Where once the Iroquois
canoed in style—
A clear liquid
caressing another name
for rock,
Now the jumping
Stretch of Avenue D
housing projects
Where Ricans and Afros
Johnny Pacheco/Wilson Pickett
The portable radio night—
Across the Domino sugar
Neon lights of the Brooklyn shore

Window carnival of
megalopolis lights
From Houston Street
Twenty kids take off
On summer bikes
Across the Williamsburg
Bridge
Their hair flying
With bodega bean protein
Below the working class
jumping like frogs—
Parrots with new raincoats
swinging canes of bamboo
Like third legs
Down diddy-bop 6th Street

of the roaring Dragons
Strollers of cool flow

When winter comes they fly
In capes down Delancey
Past the bites of pastrami
Sandwiches in Katz's
Marching through red bricks
aglow dragging hind leg
Swinging arms
Defying in simalcas

Hebrew prayers inside
metallic containers
Rolled into walls
Tenement relic
Roofs of pigeon airports

Horse-driven carts
arrive with the morning
Slicing through venetian
blinds
Along with a Polish English
Barking peaches and melons
Later the ice man a-cometh
Selling his hard water
cut into blocks
The afternoon a metallic
slide intercourses buildings
Which start to swallow
coals down their basement
Mouths.

Where did the mountains go
The immigrants ask
The place where houses

and objects went back
Into history which guided
Them into nature

Entering the roots of plants
The molasses of fruit
To become eternal again,
Now the plaster of Paris
Are the ears of the walls
The first utterances in Spanish
Recall what was left behind.

People kept arriving
as the cane fields dried
Flying bushes from another
planet
Which had a pineapple for
a moon
Vegetables and tree bark
popping out of luggage
The singers of lament
into the soul of Jacob Riis
Where the prayers of Santa Maria
Through remaining fibers
of the Torah
Eldridge Street lelolai
A Spanish never before seen
Inside gypsies.
Once Cordova the cabala
Haberdasheries of Orchard Street
Hecklers riddling bargains
Like in gone bazaars of
Some Warsaw ghetto.

Upward into the economy
Migration continues—

Out of the workers' quarters
Pieces of accents
On the ascending escalator.

The red Avenue B bus
disappearing down the
Needle holes of the garment
factories—
The drain of a city
The final sewers
Where the waste became antique
The icy winds
Of the river's edge
Stinging lower Broadway
As hot dogs
Sauerkraut and all
Gush down the pipes
of Canal

After Forsyth Park
is the beginning of Italy
Florence inside Mott
Street windows—
Palermo eyes of Angie
Flipping the big
hole of a 45 record
The Duprees dusting
Like white sugar onto
Fluffed dough—
Crisscrossing
The fire escapes
To arrive at Lourdes'
railroad flat
With knishes
she threw next to
Red beans.

Broome Street Hasidics
with Martian fur hats
With those ultimatum brims
Puerto Ricans supporting
pra-pras
Atop faces with features
Thrown out of some bag
Of universal race stew—
Mississippi rural slang
With Avenue D park view
All in exile from broken
Souths
The horses the cows the
chickens
The daisies of the rural
road
All past tense in the urbanity
that remembers
The pace of mountains
The moods of the fields.

From the guayaba bushels
outside of a town
With an Arowak name
I hear the flute shells
With the I that saw
Andalusian boats
Wash up on the beach
To distribute Moorish
eyes.

The Lower East Side
was faster than the speed
Of light
A tornado of bricks
and fire escapes
In which you had to grab

on to something or take
Off with the wayward winds—

The proletariat stoop voices
Took off like Spauldine
rubber balls
Hit by blue broomsticks
on 12th Street—
Wintertime summertime
Seasons of hallways and roofs
Between pachanga and doo-wop
A generation left
The screaming streets of
passage
Gone from the temporary
station of desire and disaster

I knew Anthony's
and Carmen
Butchy
Little Man
Eddie
Andrew
Tiny
Pichon
Vigo
Wandy
Juanito
Where are they?
The windows sucked them up
The pavement had mouths that
ate them
Urban vanishment
Illusion
I too
Henry Roth
"Call It Sleep."

Bryan Katz, "Sunrise over the city that never sleeps" (Wikimedia Commons). 2008. Used under terms of the Creative Commons Attribution-ShareAlike License.

Day

Galway Kinnell

From "The Avenue Bearing the Initial of Christ into the New World"

Was diese kleine Gasse doch für ein Reich an sich war . . .

1

pcheek pcheek pcheek pcheek pcheek
They cry. The motherbirds thieve the air
To appease them. A tug on the East River
Blasts the bass-note of its passage, lifted
From the infra-bass of the sea. A broom
Swishes over the sidewalk like feet through leaves.
Valerio's pushcart Ice Coal Kerosene
Moves   clack
                    clack
                         clack
On a broken wheelrim. Ringing in its chains
The New Star Laundry horse comes down the street
Like a roofleak whucking into a pail.
At the redlight, where a horn blares,
The Golden Harvest Bakery brakes on its gears,
Squeaks, and seethes in place. A propane-
gassed bus makes its way with big, airy sighs.

Across the street a woman throws open
Her window.
She sets, terribly softly,
Two potted plants on the windowledge
               tic   tic
And bangs shut her window.

A man leaves a doorway tic toc tic toc tic toc tic hurrah toc splat
on Avenue C tic etc and turns the corner.
Banking the same corner
A pigeon coasts 5th Street in shadows,
Looks for altitude, surmounts the rims of buildings,
And turns white.
The babybirds pipe down. It is day.

From "As Fate Would Have It"

To Rashed Hussein

On Fifth Avenue he greeted me and burst into tears.
He leaned against a wall of glass
. . . New York is without willows.
He made me cry, and water returned to it rivers.
We had coffee, and too soon went separate ways.

. . .

He was far away, vanishing
into the endless unseen.
He drank his glass like smoke,
then vanished
as a gazelle vanishes in the disappearing meadows
beneath the fog.

He stubbed his cigarette out in my heart and rested.
He didn't look at his watch,
nor was he tempted by the trees
standing tall under our tenth-floor room in Manhattan.
He was wrapped in memories, and possessed
by the ringing of a mysterious bell.
Flocks of birds and familial deaths
flap at our hands and fly away.
This is not my time.
Another winter arrived.
Mares died grazing in the distant lands.

He said: *This is not my time.*
And I gave my heart for the collapse

of cities since life's origin perhaps,
until the end of the dream.
Do we stay in this orange day going outward
just to embrace the darkness within?

Where did you come from?
A bird struck an arrow.
So I said: *She discovered my heart.*
Do we stay in this orange day going inward
just to face the harbor police?

Freed of memory, he raves.
I carry the weight of the land,
and the savior from this waywardness.
Young women shoed my soul and were gone.
Birds nested in my voice, tore me apart, then flew away.
Nothing has changed.

The songs took my place, took my place.
This is not my time.
No. This is not my homeland.
No. This is not my body.

~

As fate would have it,
an ear of wheat betrayed him
then a sparrow lead him
to the winds of the killers.

—*Translated from the Arabic by Munir Akash and Carolyn Forché*

FRANK O'HARA

A Step Away from Them

It's my lunch hour, so I go
for a walk among the hum-colored
cabs. First, down the sidewalk
where laborers feed their dirty
glistening torsos sandwiches
and Coca-Cola, with yellow helmets
on. They protect them from falling
bricks, I guess. Then onto the
avenue where skirts are flipping
above heels and blow up over
grates. The sun is hot, but the
cabs stir up the air. I look
at bargains in wristwatches. There
are cats playing in sawdust.
On

to Times Square, where the sign
blows smoke over my head, and higher
the waterfall pours lightly. A
Negro stands in a doorway with a
toothpick, languorously agitating.
A blonde chorus girl clicks: he
smiles and rubs his chin. Everything
suddenly honks: it is 12:40 of
a Thursday.
Neon in daylight is a
great pleasure, as Edwin Denby would
write, as are light bulbs in daylight.
I stop for a cheeseburger at JULIET'S
CORNER. Giulietta Masina, wife of
Federico Fellini, *è bell' attrice.*

And chocolate malted. A lady in
foxes on such a day puts her poodle
in a cab.
                    There are several Puerto
Ricans on the avenue today, which
makes it beautiful and warm. First
Bunny died, then John Latouche,
then Jackson Pollock. But is the
earth as full as life was full, of them?
And one has eaten and one walks,
past the magazines with nudes
and the posters for BULLFIGHT and
the Manhattan Storage Warehouse,
which they'll soon tear down. I
used to think they had the Armory
Show there.
                    A glass of papaya juice
and back to work. My heart is in my
pocket, it is Poems by Pierre Reverdy.

MEREDITH SHEPARD

Why I Hate New York

It's the number that gets me.
Immigrants sweeping streets, I expect—but
so many? And the old white face
with pockmarks like crater holes in the moon
standing outside Port Authority
crack addict, maybe, because he's
with young men who look like they can run
and hate me because I don't know a thing
about this city, all I have is my ticket out.

I can't hear the women's high heels
through the bus window, but they look bitchy,
too high, too thin, too sharp to be passing without stopping
the ones I've just noticed looking poor together.

Every iron seat is taken at an outdoor plaza. March,
one of the first sunny days,
of course New Yorkers want to eat paninis
with their paled mouths in open air
but there are so many together the only differences
between suit, suit, suit-skirt are tie-colors,
hair waviness, whether they're wearing sneakers.

Women pictured on bus stops selling clothes and sex
plaster themselves apart from the rest.
The goal of any artist, to be noticed and apart
for beauty. Even if they are no longer real.

The handwritten sign above the Chinese/Korean
driver's head, *We drivers depend your tips,*
Thank You!!!
I wonder how much minimum wage is, and pull out a few bucks.

There are people like me who have not come to New York
for New York. We buy food in the airport and wait.
The Ethiopians, the Indonesians, the local blacks
sweep through.
No matter how long we are delayed here,
there is always another shift.

Luis Cabalquinto ~

August Walk

I'm walking westbound on Fourteenth Street
to grab a late lunch at a Subway fastfood shop.
It's unseasonably cool for the middle of August.
Two panhandlers at the corner on First Avenue
are busy working the thick pedestrian traffic—

when it hits me: I'm 7,000 miles away from home,
all the way to the other side of the world.
Does it matter after thirty years? Many city places
I've also called "home": this self-declared planetary
citizen feels at home anywhere his foot touches ground.

I'll wager on this one for the future: we're all
going to end up world citizens, freely crossing
boundaries; simply—"Earthniks" of the universe!
I look up, assured by the same light blue sky from
my boyhood, the same rolling cloud that haunt us.

I go in for my daily veggie sandwich, no cheese.
If I keep this up I'll lose another ugly ten pounds.
Twenty off should be about right, enough to bring me
to the creation of that long-awaited world government.
I'm getting ready to give up my current passport.

Purvi Shah

Made in India, Immigrant Song #3
(a note from a New York City streetwalker)

Some worker in the sweat
of Madras, some former weaver
from Kashmir, some hand in Ahmadabad's dust,
has been pounding iron again.

The New York City streets swell with feet;
multihued tracks glide over the flat steel
disks which offer entry into the city's interior
lairs. The writing seeps through our soles
though few fathom the signature, "Made
in India." These alien

metal coins, transported
like my birth, mask
a labyrinth of tunnels
in a city where origin
and destination are confused.
Sometimes I wear the stamp
on myself; sometimes I feel
the wear of a surrounding world erase
the fine etchings. Here the imprint

of India is a traveler's
mutation: the body's chamber is made
hole, the skin not smooth, circular,
but cloaking a bumpy network
of channels, spirit mobile, expanding.

NICANOR PARRA

Resurrection

One day in a park in New York City
A pigeon fell at my feet
She thrashed 4 a few seconds
And then died
But the most unexpected thing of all
Was that she revived on the spot
Without giving me time to react
And took off flying
As though she had never been dead at all

Bells were ringing somewhere far away

And I just stood there watching her zigzag and zigzag
Between the marble statues
& there was a noisy growling in my guts
& I got started spitting out this poem

—Translated from the Spanish by Liz Werner

E. E. CUMMINGS

"at the ferocious phenomenon"

at the ferocious phenomenon of 5 o'clock i find myself gently decomposing in the mouth of New York. Between its supple financial teeth deliriously sprouting from complacent gums, a morsel prettily wanders buoyed on the murderous saliva of industry. the morsel is i.

Vast cheeks enclose me.

a gigantic uvula with imperceptible gesticulations threatens the tubular downward blackness occasionally from which detaching itself bumps clumsily into the throat A meticulous vulgarity:

a sodden fastidious normal explosion; a square murmur, a winsome flatulence—

In the soft midst of the tongue sits the Woolworth building a serene pastile-shaped insipid kinesis or frail swooping lozenge. a ruglike sentience whose papillæ expertly drink the docile perpendicular taste of this squirming cube of undiminished silence, supports while devouring the firm tumult of exquisitely insecure sharp algebraic music. For the first time in sorting from this vast nonchalant inward walk of volume the flat minute gallop of careful hugeness i am conjugated by the sensual mysticism of entire vertical being, i am skilfully construed by a delicately experimenting colossus whose irrefutable spiral antics involve me with the soothings of plastic hypnotism . i am accurately parsed by this gorgeous rush of upward lips. . . .

cleverly

perching on the sudden extremity of one immense tooth myself surveys safely the complete important profane frantic inconsequential gastronomic mystery of mysteries

, life.

Far below myself the lunging leer of horizontal large distinct ecstasy wags and. rages Laughters jostle grins nudge smiles push—. deep into the edgeless gloaming gladness hammers incessant putrid spikes of madness (at

Myself's height these various innocent ferocities are superseded by the sole prostituted ferocity of silence, it is) still 5 o'clock
I stare only always into the tremendous canyon the

, tremendous canyon always only exhales a climbing dark exact walloping human noise of digestible millions whose rich slovenly obscene procession always floats through the thin amorous enormous only lips of the evening

And it is 5 o'clock

in the oblong air, from which a singular ribbon of common sunset is hanging,

snow speaks slowly

Shokry Eldaly

I Had This Dream/the city of shadows

I had this dream where I was in the
Cockpit of a Seven-Forty-Seven
Flying over the city of shadows,
Looking down through the window
At the five boroughs of the Ghetto,
Flicking switches and dropping
Paradise bombs.

In this dream
The plane is trembling with every
Payload as, beneath me, swells
Of light and smoke erupt, hydrants combust,
And liquid color—hues like an automatic has met
An ink cartridge—are being showered through the air
As the shadows retract and burn like
New Rome, New Sodom, New Gomorrah,
With all the wrath of a love letter ablaze.

Ejected from the plane,
I fall through cross fire
Of brick and rock.
All around me shatterings
Drag 'cross ground and return to
Unabandon the buildings they'd left.

Paint chips and ashes are streaming
From babies' mouths and
Covering gang signs on walls with
Murals that depict a house of reunion.

In empty forgotten lots,
Colorful *casitas* and
Salsero skeletons carrying
Maracas, *congas*, trumpets,
Timbales and guitars
Spring up like wild flowers.

And the ground, all day long, keeps glowing
Like a new born Sun looking to show off.

Later, when night falls and
The streets have had their fill,
The only darknesses that stand are
That of the opulence of night and the silhouettes
Of celebration, cast for television moments
By the warm and glowing streetlights.

The tenements are lit up like jukeboxes, dancing and
Bellowing through their neon colored mouths
Music of hope and salvation.
Even the saplings are beginning to revel and sway as
The music formerly played in ear buds
And above kitchen sinks in the backs of restaurants,
And in factories at low forgettable tones,
Now coming forth from the lips of windowsills,
Increases in volume and vigor as
They transition from *boleros* of hope
To songs of Deliverance.
The notes and rhythmic beats
Striking and reverberating against the formerly
Bare-boxed windowsill cemeteries are
Birthing gardens and vines that scale the buildings,
Fill the apartments and stretch out onto lampposts,
Before reaching down and lending
The homeless heart-healing ambrosias that
They've neither seen, nor spoke, nor heard of.

As I walk, cornflakes are falling from
Dizzying heights like snow.

The people above are
Emptying their cupboards,
And crying the words
"I will not eat you anymore!"

As citizens below prepare
pasteles, platanos, tamales, y yuca
There are some leaning out of windows,
Shouting victory cries and
Praying thanks to God, whilst others
Use their lips to throw love onto the street.

There are two, in the middle, posing for a picture.
The *viejo* hands his delicate flower a hibiscus (*maga*),
As he, like a soldier home from war,
Holds the small of her back and dips her.

Anyone who can—
Speak is singing
Move is dancing
Feel is touching

Walking now through sugarcane valleys
My toes are digging ground
Where asphalt once suffocated earth.

People around me are lifting coconuts to their mouths,
They're laughing before bonfires that are
Burning friendly in the warm fragrant night.

By the curb, babies coo as they
Look at themselves in the reflections
Of fire hydrant rivers.

A little one,
In the same shoes she's worn for too long
To school, to church, to bed,
Motions for me to help her take them off.

After freeing the clasp
Of her white leather shackle,
I look up to see that she's turned into a woman.

She points with a smile,
Down an empty street,
Before taking my hand.
Leading me the first few steps,
Our hands part from one another
As I see beside an open hydrant
An old leather chair,
Like the one that used to
Sit beside the bath in my
Grandmother's washroom,
I begin walking quickly.

From the seat of the chair,
I pick up my bar of olive oil soap,
And wash my hair in the hydrant and
Watch as the last bits of yesterday
Drip into the gutter
As my curls grow long.

Looking down I can hear the voices of family,
And so I hesitate to lift my head.
On my shoulder is the warm hand
Of the woman
With a birthmark like her mother's.
I look up, and before me is
The house I grew up in

And my child who
Only got to breathe the air of the world
For but a moment
Before joining her mother
In slumber.

She looks at me
And I hold her, bury myself into her,

And she says to me,
"Yes, Papa, it's true. There is Home again."

DAVID SEMANKI

Rain

Yesterday was the last day of summer.
And it makes sense
you weren't with me

then. Or even
on this rainy afternoon—

you're teaching me to live
apart from you, which has reduced to

breakfast dishes crowding the nightstand,
the TV droning with some Julie Christie drama,
my black hair unwashed for a fifth day.

After all what's grief to someone
Who never tires of longing
except a manner of existing
in the present, where nothing is derivative.

Strange. It's much easier now
to reconcile
the scene of when I first saw you—

crossing a city street on a busy September afternoon.
The one perfect moment, before language.

ROBERT LOWELL

Central Park

Scaling small rocks, exhaling smog,
gasping at game-scents like a dog,
now light as pollen, now as white
and winded as a grounded kite—
I watched the lovers occupy
every inch of earth and sky:
one figure of geometry,
multiplied to infinity,
straps down, and sunning openly . . .
each precious, public, pubic tangle
an equilateral triangle,
lost in the park, half covered by
the shade of some low stone or tree.
The stain of fear and poverty
spread through each trapped anatomy,
and darkened every mote of dust.
All wished to leave this drying crust,
borne on the delicate wings of lust
like bees, and cast their fertile drop
into the overwhelming cup.

Drugged and humbled by the smell
of zoo-straw mixed with animal,
the lion prowled his slummy cell,
serving his life-term in jail—
glaring, grinding, on his heel,
with tingling step and testicle . . .

Behind a dripping rock, I found
a one-day kitten on the ground—

deprived, weak, ignorant and blind,
squeaking, tubular, left behind—
dying with its deserter's rich
Welfare lying out of reach:
milk cartons, kidney heaped to spoil,
two plates sheathed with silver foil.

Shadows had stained the afternoon;
high in an elm, a snagged balloon
wooed the attraction of the moon.
Scurrying from the mouth of night,
a single, fluttery, paper kite
grazed Cleopatra's Needle, and sailed
where the light of the sun had failed.
Then night, the night—the jungle hour,
The rich in his slit-windowed tower . . .
Old Pharaohs starving in your foxholes,
with painted banquets on the walls,
fists knotted in your captives' hair,
tyrants with little food to spare—
all your embalming left you mortal,
glazed, black, and hideously eternal,
all your plunder and gold leaf
only served to draw the thief . . .

We beg delinquents for our life.
Behind each bush, perhaps a knife;
each landscaped crag, each flowering shrub,
hides a policeman with a club.

Durs Grünbein

From "Peacocks on Broadway"

III

December cold, and the sun is burning on the furs
Of the old ladies in Central Park, one wearing
Sneakers with her coat, another cowboy boots.
And they are all ennobled in this light
The sea wind purifies, a Magnum filter making
Whatever's small much bigger and whatever's big
Into something quickly lost to sight, up to
The sky, or down the rows of houses. Why look up
When the unusual wanders the streets
As one of many themes
Of the music of this city. Andante cantabile,
Its feathers dragging, its little crown aslant
On its head, a peacock walked through the crowd,
And another peacock, and then another—
Three slowly striding, turkey-footed divas.
Where from? Where to? The people from Harlem
Knew that no more than the people from Queens.
No zoo had lost them, nor had the secret
Herb garden of the Neogothic cathedral.
Decadence could be had here cheap, an offer
Made in passing: three for the price of one.
Broadway took them, like everything that moves.

—Translated from the German by Andrew Shields

Sharon Olds

Summer Solstice, New York City

By the end of the longest day of the year he could not stand it,
he went up the iron stairs through the roof of the building
and over the soft, tarry surface
to the edge, put one leg over the complex green tin cornice
and said if they came a step closer that was it.
Then the huge machinery of the earth began to work for his life,
the cops came in their suits blue-grey as the sky on a cloudy evening
and one put on a bullet-proof vest, a
black shell around his own life,
life of his children's father, in case
the man was armed, and one, slung with a
rope like the sign of his bounden duty,
came up out of a hole in the top of the neighboring building
like the gold hole they say is in the top of the head,
and began to lurk toward the man who wanted to die.
The tallest cop approached him directly,
softly, slowly, talking to him, talking, talking,
while the man's leg hung over the lip of the next world
and the crowd gathered in the street, silent, and the
hairy net with its implacable grid was
unfolded near the curb and spread out and
stretched as the sheet is prepared to receive at a birth.
Then they all came a little closer
where he squatted next to his death, his shirt
glowing its milky glow like something
growing in a dish at night in the dark in a lab and then
everything stopped
as his body jerked and he
stepped down from the parapet and went toward them
and they closed in on him, I thought they were going to

beat him up, as a mother whose child has been
lost will scream at the child when it's found, they
took him by the arms and held him up and
leaned him against the wall of the chimney and the
tall cop lit a cigarette
in his own mouth, and gave it to him, and
then they all lit cigarettes, and the
red, glowing ends burned like the
tiny campfires we lit at night
back at the beginning of the world.

Martín Espada ~

The Mexican Cabdriver's Poem for His Wife, Who Has Left Him

We were sitting in traffic
on the Brooklyn Bridge,
so I asked the poets
in the backseat of my cab
to write a poem for you.

They asked
if you are like the moon
or the trees.

I said no,
she is like the bridge
when there is so much traffic
I have time
to watch the boats
on the river.

Marilyn Bridges, "Lane Manned, New York City 1985," © Marilyn Bridges 1985. Gelatin silver print. Herbert F. Johnson Museum of Art, Cornell University, Permanent Collection. Gift of Paula J. Mueller. Used by permission of the photographer.

Evening

Nikki Giovanni

The New Yorkers

In front of the bank building
after six o'clock the gathering
of the bag people begins

In cold weather they huddle
around newspapers
when it is freezing they get
cardboard boxes

Someone said they are all rich eccentrics
Someone is   of course   crazy

The man and his buddy moved
to the truck port
in the adjoining building
most early evenings he visits
his neighbors awaiting
the return of his friend
from points unknown to me
they seem to be a spontaneous
combustion these night people
they evaporate during the light of day
only to emerge at evening glow
as if they had never been away

I am told there are people
who live underground
in the layer between the subways
and the pipes that run them
they have harnessed the steam

to heat their corner
and cook their food
though there is no electricity
making them effectively   moles

The twentieth century has been
    two big wars and two small ones
    the automobile and the SST
    telephones and satellites in the sky
    man on the moon and spacecraft on Jupiter
How odd to also see the people
of New York City living
in the doorways of public buildings
as if this is an emerging nation
though of course it is

Look at the old woman
who sits on 57th Street and 8th Avenue
selling pencils
I don't know where she spends the night
she sits summer and winter
snow or rain humming
some white religious song
she must weigh over 250 pounds
the flesh on her legs has stretched
like a petite pair of stockings
onto a medium frame
beyond its ability to fit
there are tears and holes
of various purples in her legs
things and stuff ooze from them
drying and running again
there is never   though   a smell
she does not ask you to buy
a pencil nor will her eyes

condemn your health
it's easy really to walk by her
unlike the man in front
of Tiffany's she holds her pencils
near her knee
you take or not
depending upon your writing needs

He on the other hand is blind and walking
his german shepherd dog
his sign says THERE
BUT FOR THE GRACE OF GOD
GOES YOU and there is a long
explanation of his condition
It's rather easy for the Tiffany shopper
to see his condition
  he is Black

Uptown on 125th Street is an old blind Black woman
she is out only in good
  weather and clothes
her house is probably spotless
as southern ladies are wont to keep house
and her wig is always on straight
  You got something for me, she called
  What do you want, I asked
  What's yo name? I know yo family
  No, you don't, I said laughing   You don't know
  anything about me
  You that Eyetalian poet ain't you? I know yo voice. I seen
  you on television
I peered closely into her eyes
  You didn't see me or you'd know I'm black
  Let me feel yo hair   if you Black   Hold down yo head

I did and she did
  Got something for me, she laughed
  You felt my hair   that's good luck
  Good luck is money, chile   she said
  Good luck is money

MacDougal Street

As I went walking up and down to take the evening air,
  (Sweet to meet upon the street, why must I be so shy?)
I saw him lay his hand upon her torn black hair;
  ("Little dirty Latin child, let the lady by!")

The women squatting on the stoops were slovenly and fat,
  (Lay me out in organdie, lay me out in lawn!)
And everywhere I stepped there was a baby or a cat;
  (Lord, God in Heaven, will it never be dawn?)

The fruit-carts and clam-carts were ribald as a fair,
  (Pink nets and wet shells trodden under heel)
She had haggled from the fruit-man of his rotting ware;
  (I shall never get to sleep, the way I feel!)

He walked like a king through the filth and the clutter,
  (Sweet to meet upon the street, why did you glance me by?)
But he caught the quaint Italian quip she flung him from the gutter;
  (What can there be to cry about that I should lie and cry?)

He laid his darling hand upon her little black head,
  (I wish I were a ragged child with ear-rings in my ears!)
And he said she was a baggage to have said what she had said;
  (Truly I shall be ill unless I stop these tears!)

Allen Ginsberg

From "Mugging"

I

Tonite I walked out of my red apartment door on East tenth street's dusk—
Walked out of my home ten years, walked out in my honking neighborhood
Tonite at seven walked out past garbage cans chained to concrete anchors
Walked under black painted fire escapes, giant castiron plate covering a hole in ground
—Crossed the street, traffic lite red, thirteen bus roaring by liquor store,
past corner pharmacy iron grated, past Coca Cola & Mylai posters fading scraped on brick
Past Chinese Laundry wood door'd, & broken cement stoop steps
For Rent hall painted green & purple Puerto Rican style
Along E. 10th's glass splattered pavement, kid blacks & Spanish oiled hair adolescents' crowded house fronts—
Ah, tonite I walked out on my block NY City under humid summer sky Halloween,
thinking what happened Timothy Leary joining brain police for a season?
thinking what's all this Weathermen, secrecy & selfrighteousness beyond reason—F.B.I. plots?
Walked past a taxicab controlling the bottle strewn curb—
past young fellows with their umbrella handles & canes leaning against a ravaged Buick
—and as I looked at the crowd of kids on the stoop—a boy stepped up, put his arm around my neck
tenderly I thought for a moment, squeezed harder, his umbrella handle against my skull,

and his friends took my arm, a young brown companion tripped
his foot 'gainst my ankle—
as I went down shouting Om Ah Hūṃ to gangs of lovers on
the stoop watching
slowly appreciating, why this is a raid, these strangers mean strange
business
with what—my pockets, bald head, broken-healed-bone leg, my
softshoes, my heart—
Have they knives? Om Ah Hūṃ—Have they sharp metal wood
to shove in eye ear ass? Om Ah Hūṃ
& slowly reclined on the pavement, struggling to keep my woolen
bag of poetry address calendar & Leary-lawyer notes hung
from my shoulder
dragged in my neat orlon shirt over the crossbar of a broken
metal door
dragged slowly onto the fire-soiled floor an abandoned store,
laundry candy counter 1929—
now a mess of papers & pillows & plastic car seat covers cracked
cockroach-corpsed ground—
my wallet back pocket passed over the iron foot step guard
and fell out, stole by God Muggers' lost fingers, Strange—
Couldn't tell—snakeskin wallet actually plastic, 70 dollars my bank
money for a week,
old broken wallet—and dreary plastic contents—Amex card &
Manf. Hanover Trust Credit too—business card from Mr. Spears
British Home Minister Drug Squad—my draft card—member-
ship ACLU & Naropa Institute Instructor's identification
Om Ah Hūṃ I continued chanting Om Ah Hūṃ
Putting my palm on the neck of an 18 year old boy fingering
my back pocket crying "Where's the money"
"Om Ah Hūṃ there isn't any"
My card Chief Boo-Hoo Neo American Church New Jersey &
Lower East Side
Om Ah Hūṃ—what not forgotten crowded wallet—Mobil
Credit, Shell? old lovers addresses on cardboard pieces, book-
sellers calling cards—

—"Shut up or we'll murder you"—"Om Ah Hūṃ take it easy"
Lying on the floor shall I shout more loud?—the metal door closed on blackness
one boy felt my broken healed ankle, looking for hundred dollar bills behind my stocking weren't even there—a third boy untied my Seiko Hong Kong watch rough from right wrist leaving a claspprick skin tiny bruise
"Shut up and we'll get out of here"—and so they left,
as I rose from the cardboard mattress thinking Om Ah Hūṃ didn't stop em enough,
the tone of voice too loud—my shoulder bag with 10,000 dollars full of poetry left on the broken floor—

JOHN HOLLANDER ~

From "New York"

West in Manhattan where the sun has set
The elevator rises calmly yet
In my dark tower, against the tower-dimmed sky,
Whose wide, old windows yield my narrower eye
Images no revision can defeat:
Newspapers blown along the empty street
At three A.M. (somewhere in between 'odd,'
A guru told me long ago, and 'God');
Calm steam rising from manholes in the dark;
Clean asphalt of an avenue; the spark
Of gold in every mica window high
On westward faces of the peaks; the sky
Near dawn, framed in the zig-zag canyon rim
Of cross-streets; bits of distant bridge, the dim
Lustrous ropes of pale lights dipping low;
Rivers unseen beneath, sable and slow.

February Evening in New York

As the stores close, a winter light
    opens air to iris blue,
    glint of frost through the smoke,
    grains of mica, salt of the sidewalk.
As the buildings close, released autonomous
    feet pattern the streets
    in hurry and stroll; balloon heads
    drift and dive above them; the bodies
    aren't really there.
As the lights brighten, as the sky darkens,
    a woman with crooked heels says to another woman
    while they step along at a fair pace,
    'You know, I'm telling you, what I love best
    is life. I love life! Even if I ever get
    to be old and wheezy—or limp! You know?
    Limping along?—I'd still . . .' Out of hearing.
To the multiple disordered tones
    of gears changing, a dance
    to the compass points, out, four-way river.
    Prospect of sky
    wedged into avenues, left at the ends of streets,
    west sky, east sky: more life tonight! A range
    of open time at winter's outskirts.

Anne Pierson Wiese

Body Elite

For years I belonged to a neighborhood gym
in Brooklyn: a brownstone transformed, crooked floors
and all, by weight machines, rubber matting,
turquoise paint galore, a youthful staff eating
take-out from the Italian place next door.
I'd thread my way between body builders
taut and ornery as prize boars, performing
my 20-pound reps, invisible, as I assumed.

When I moved to Manhattan I dropped the gym,
but emerging from the subway one evening
I glimpsed a man I recognized, a silent
lifter of light weights who never socialized—
compact of body and purpose—whose face
in the crowd shone back like a private moon.

Schubertiana

1

In the evening darkness in a place outside New York, a viewpoint
where one single glance will encompass the homes of eight
million people.
The giant city becomes a long shimmering drift, a spiral galaxy
seen from the side.
Within the galaxy coffee cups are pushed across the counter, the
shop windows beg from passersby, a flurry of shoes leave no
prints.
The climbing fire escapes, elevator doors glide shut, behind
police-locked doors a perpetual seethe of voices.
Slouched bodies doze in subway cars, the hurtling catacombs.
I know too—without statistics—that right now Schubert is being
played in a room over there and that for someone the notes
are more real than anything else.

2

The endless expanses of the human brain are crumpled to the
size of a fist.
In April the swallow returns to last year's nest under the guttering
of this very barn in this very parish.
She flies from Transvaal, passes the equator, flies for six weeks
over two continents, makes for precisely this vanishing dot in
the land-mass.
And the man who catches the signals from a whole life in a few
ordinary chords for five strings,
who makes a river flow through the eye of a needle,
is a stout young gentleman from Vienna known to his friends as
"The Mushroom," who slept with his glasses on
and stood at his writing desk punctually in the morning.

And then the wonderful centipedes of his manuscript were set
in motion.

3

The string quintet is playing. I walk home through warm forests
with the ground springy under me,
curl up like an embryo, fall asleep, roll weightless into the future,
suddenly feel that the plants have thoughts.

4

So much we have to trust, simply to live through our daily day
without sinking through the earth!
Trust the piled snow clinging to the mountain slope above the
village.
Trust the promises of silence and the smile of understanding, trust
that the accident telegram isn't for us and that the sudden
axe-blow from within won't come.
Trust the axles that carry us on the highway in the middle of
the three hundred times life-size bee swarm of steel.
But none of this is really worth our confidence.
The five strings say we can trust something else. And they keep
us com pany part of the way.
As when the time-switch clicks off in the stairwell and the
fingers—trustingly—follow the blind handrail that finds its
way in the darkness.

5

We squeeze together at the piano and play with four hands in
F minor, two coachmen on the same coach, it looks a little
ridiculous.
The hands seem to be moving resonant weights to and fro, as if
we were tampering with the counterweights
in an effort to disturb the great scale arm's terrible balance: joy
and suffering weighing exactly the same.
Annie said, "This music is so heroic," and she's right.

But those whose eyes enviously follow men of action, who secretly despise themselves for not being murderers,
don't recognize themselves here,
and the many who buy and sell people and believe that everyone can be bought, don't recognize themselves here.
Not their music. The long melody that remains itself in all its transformations, sometimes glittering and pliant, sometimes rugged and strong, snail track and steel wire.
The perpetual humming that follows us—now—
up
the depths.

—*Translated from the Swedish by Robin Fulton*

Herman Spector

Wiseguy Type

The smart little gent with the shoebutton eyes
and the folded nose, twice-over, so;
with the diffident smile, and the spectacles
like a hornèd owl, so wise, so wise,

Is a sharpshooter born in a cabaret to a rattle
of drums and a spastic shudder;
By a pinkish floozie with powdered thighs,
and a monocled punk in a cutaway,
And a tinhorn song, and a clicking jig,
and a swift, pat fade
and a getaway . . .

Is a wise, wise baby who won't take sides,
playing the middle against the ends;
shuffles the cards with a crack and a flutter,
looks sharp in the dark for omens and friends,
Concedes with a mutter, You may be right.
It may be true but I can't decide,
If the cards are stacked then what does it matter?
If death is the answer, what's the use?
I'm a lonesome wolf in a cold, hard winter, he says
And the rest is up to Youse.

Jessica Hagedorn

Latin Music in New York

made me dance with you
tito   eddie   n ray
somewhere with plumjam eyelids
i danced with you
in a roomful of mirrors
in miss harlow's house

the white girl's in town
and i smell death
the poet dying in a bar
body shaking in time
to lady day's song
    he's dying in a nod
    in a lullaby
    of ambulance haze
    and chloral hydrate
    they burned his brain

somewhere
i saw the white girl smiling
la cucaracha was up all night
hiding her spoons   her mirrors   her revolutions
in the morning
            the trace of vampires
            still there
            in the blood   even after a bath

you can't wash it away
you can't hide it
again and again

i looked under my bed
     inside a perfume box
          in the argentinian dagger
               the baby wolf gave me
                    in your eyes
                         in a furtive smile
                              in a good fuck
                                   in the boogaloo i do
there's no escaping it
     somewhere   with plumjam eyelids

i danced the tasty freeze shuffle with you
the reds   the blues   the tango con tu madre
it's there
in town for the night
a guest appearance   a quick solo
death gets hyped
and i'm in love again

latin music in new york
made me dance with you
azúcar y chocolaté
the alligator dream
of a tropical night

death makes a quick run
to las vegas
trying to take the poet
with him

latin music in new york
made me dance with you
tito   eddie   n ray

revolutions are creeping out
from under my bed!

and i sing a song for you
and you
and
you

Broadway

I shall never forget you, Broadway
Your golden and calling lights.

I'll remember you long,
Tall-walled river of rush and play.

Hearts that know you hate you
And lips that have given you laughter
Have gone to their ashes of life and its roses,
Cursing the dreams that were lost
In the dust of your harsh and trampled stones.

Vachel Lindsay

A Rhyme about an Electrical Advertising Sign

I look on the specious electrical light
Blatant, mechanical, crawling and white,
Wickedly red or malignantly green
Like the beads of a young Senegambian queen.
Showing, while millions of souls hurry on,
The virtues of collars, from sunset till dawn,
By dart or by tumble of whirl within whirl,
Starting new fads for the shame-weary girl,
By maggoty motions in sickening line
Proclaiming a hat or a soup or a wine,
While there far above the steep cliffs of the street

The stars sing a message elusive and sweet.
Now man cannot rest in his pleasure and toil
His clumsy contraptions of coil upon coil
Till the thing he invents, in its use and its range,
Leads on to the marvelous CHANGE BEYOND CHANGE
Some day this old Broadway shall climb to the skies,
As a ribbon of cloud on a soul-wind shall rise
And we shall be lifted, rejoicing by night,
Till we join with the planets who choir their delight.
The signs in the streets and the signs in the skies
Shall make a new Zodiac, guiding the wise,
And Broadway make one with that marvelous stair
That is climbed by the rainbow-clad spirits of prayer.

W. H. Auden

September 1, 1939

I sit in one of the dives
On Fifty-second Street
Uncertain and afraid
As the clever hopes expire
Of a low dishonest decade:
Waves of anger and fear
Circulate over the bright
And darkened lands of the earth,
Obsessing our private lives;
The unmentionable odour of death
Offends the September night.

Accurate scholarship can
Unearth the whole offence
From Luther until now
That has driven a culture mad,
Find what occurred at Linz,
What huge imago made
A psychopathic god:
I and the public know
What all schoolchildren learn,
Those to whom evil is done
Do evil in return.

Exiled Thucydides knew
All that a speech can say
About Democracy,
And what dictators do,
The elderly rubbish they talk
To an apathetic grave;
Analyzed all in his book,

The enlightenment driven away,
The habit-forming pain,
Mismanagement and grief:
We must suffer them all again.

Into this neutral air
Where blind skyscrapers use
Their full height to proclaim
The strength of Collective Man,
Each language pours its vain
Competitive excuse:
But who can live for long
In an euphoric dream;
Out of the mirror they stare,
Imperialism's face
And the international wrong.

Faces along the bar
Cling to their average day:
The lights must never go out,
The music must always play,
All the conventions conspire
To make this fort assume
The furniture of home;
Lest we should see where we are,
Lost in a haunted wood,
Children afraid of the night
Who have never been happy or good.

The windiest militant trash
Important Persons shout
Is not so crude as our wish:
What mad Nijinsky wrote:
About Diaghilev
Is true of the normal heart;
For the error bred in the bone

Of each woman and each man
Craves what it cannot have,
Not universal love
But to be loved alone.

From the conservative dark
Into the ethical life
The dense commuters come,
Repeating their morning vow;
"I will be true to the wife,
I'll concentrate more on my work,"
And helpless governors wake
To resume their compulsory game:
Who can release them now,
Who can reach the deaf,
Who can speak for the dumb?

All I have is a voice
To undo the folded lie,
The romantic lie in the brain
Of the sensual man-in-the-street
And the lie of Authority
Whose buildings grope the sky:
There is no such thing as the State
And no one exists alone;
Hunger allows no choice
To the citizen or the police;
We must love one another or die.

Defenseless under the night
Our world in stupor lies;
Yet, dotted everywhere,
Ironic points of light
Flash out wherever the Just
Exchange their messages:
May I, composed like them

Of Eros and of dust,
Beleaguered by the same
Negation and despair,
Show an affirming flame.

Hart Crane

To Brooklyn Bridge

How many dawns, chill from his rippling rest
The seagull's wings shall dip and pivot him,
Shedding white rings of tumult, building high
Over the chained bay waters Liberty—

Then, with inviolate curve, forsake our eyes
As apparitional as sails that cross
Some page of figures to be filed away;
—Till elevators drop us from our day . . .

I think of cinemas, panoramic sleights
With multitudes bent toward some flashing scene
Never disclosed, but hastened to again,
Foretold to other eyes on the same screen;

And Thee, across the harbor, silver-paced
As though the sun took step of thee, yet left
Some motion ever unspent in thy stride,—
Implicitly thy freedom staying thee!

Out of some subway scuttle, cell or loft
A bedlamite speeds to thy parapets,
Tilting there momently, shrill shirt ballooning,
A jest falls from the speechless caravan.

Down Wall, from girder into street noon leaks,
A rip-tooth of the sky's acetylene;
All afternoon the cloud-flown derricks turn . . .
Thy cables breathe the North Atlantic still.

And obscure as that heaven of the Jews,
Thy guerdon . . . Accolade thou dost bestow
Of anonymity time cannot raise:
Vibrant reprieve and pardon thou dost show.

O harp and altar, of the fury fused,
(How could mere toil align thy choiring strings!)
Terrific threshold of the prophet's pledge,
Prayer of pariah, and the lover's cry,—

Again the traffic lights that skim thy swift
Unfractioned idiom, immaculate sigh of stars,
Beading thy path—condense eternity:
And we have seen night lifted in thine arms.

Under thy shadow by the piers I waited;
Only in darkness is thy shadow clear.
The City's fiery parcels all undone,
Already snow submerges an iron year . . .

O Sleepless as the river under thee,
Vaulting the sea, the prairies' dreaming sod,
Unto us lowliest sometime sweep, descend
And of the curveship lend a myth to God.

Willie Perdomo

123rd Street Rap

A day on
123rd Street

goes a little
something like
this:

Automatic bullets bounce
off stoop steps

It's about time to pay
all my debts

Church bells bong for
drunken mourners

Baby men growing on
all the corners

Money that
ain't mine

Sun that
don't shine

Trees that
don't grow

Wind that
won't blow

Drug posses
ready to rumble

Ceiling starting
to crumble

Abuelas close
eyes and pray

While they watch
the children play

Not much I
can say

Except day turns
to night

And I can't tell what's
wrong from what's right

on 123rd Street

Lucien Clergue, "Night in New York, from portfolio SURVEY 1986," 1977. Gelatin silver print. Photo © Lucien Clergue/SAIF, Paris/VAGA, New York. Herbert F. Johnson Museum of Art, Cornell University, Permanent Collection. Gift of Sheldon and Carol Sobel. Used by permission of the photographer.

Night

Walt Whitman

When I Heard at the Close of the Day

When I heard at the close of the day how my name had been
receiv'd with plaudits in the capitol, still it was not a happy
night for me that follow'd,
And else when I carous'd, or when my plans were accomplish'd,
still I was not happy,
But the day when I rose at dawn from the bed of perfect health,
refresh'd, singing, inhaling the ripe breath of autumn,
When I saw the full moon in the west grow pale and disappear
in the morning light,
When I wander'd alone over the beach, and undressing bathed,
laughing with the cool waters, and saw the sun rise,
And when I thought how my dear friend my lover was on his
way coming, O then I was happy,
O then each breath tasted sweeter, and all that day my food
nourish'd me more, and the beautiful day pass'd well,
And the next came with equal joy, and with the next at evening
came my friend,
And that night while all was still I heard the waters roll slowly
continually up the shores,
I heard the hissing rustle of the liquid and sands as directed to
me whispering to congratulate me,
For the one I love most lay sleeping by me under the same cover
in the cool night,
In the stillness in the autumn moonbeams his face was inclined
toward me,
And his arm lay lightly around my breast—and that night I was
happy.

Anna Margolin

Evening on Fifth Avenue

I
It's April
and the pure stroke of a bell.
The street is raised up
on fiery hands
to the ebbing day.

How beautiful, how sad, the faces are.

It is April's sorrow,
black processions of cars,
pale, lightly-rustling clothing,
and on the marble steps of the hotel—
people set like gemstones
of delicate, idyllic, shining light.

2
Over the dusky avenue,
in the violet mist of the avenue
iridescent butterflies
flutter.

Limousines
float along the avenue
like mysterious ships,
and the raw shriek of sirens hangs
threateningly.

Carrying night in their eyes,
night and destruction and gold in their eyes,

like poems lulling themselves, young women stroll
and nervously spread their small wings
over the avenue
like demented butterflies.

—*Translated from the Yiddish by Shirley Kumove*

Gwendolyn Bennett

Street Lamps in Early Spring

Night wears a garment
All velvet soft, all violet blue . . .
And over her face she draws a veil
As shimmering fine as floating dew . . .
And here and there
In the black of her hair
The subtle hands of Night
Move slowly with their gem-starred light.

Tom Sleigh

From "New York American Spell, 2001"

I / OMEN

What was going on in the New York American
Black/red/green helmeted neon night?
The elevator door was closing behind us, we were the ones

Plunging floor after floor after floor after floor
To the abyss—but it was someone else's face
Staring from the screen out at us, someone else's face

Saying something flashing from the teleprompter:
Though what the face said was meant to reassure,
Down in the abyss the footage kept playing,

All of it looping back like children chanting
The answers to nonsensical riddles, taunting
A classmate who doesn't know the question:

"Because it's too far to walk" "Time to get a new fence"
"A big red rock eater." And as the images rewound
And the face kept talking, the clear night sky

Filled up with smoke and the smoke kept pouring
Itself out into the air like a voice saying something
It can't stop saying, some murky omen

Like school kids asking: "Why do birds fly south?"
"What time is it when an elephant sits on the fence?"
"What's big, red and eats rocks?"

Melanie Rehak

Autobiography: New York

Returning alone after long absence
I was engulfed. No novel, no play
had prepared me for this,
the arched November trees
glazed with ice, the night-emptied
sidewalks chipped with mica
in silent offering.
I had left it all behind
and here—it rose! *The City's*
fiery parcels all undone.

It was the season of regret
and the great wave of first
love lost swept over me.
Catching the buildings'
hooded eyes from afar—
my true paramours!—I was
mournful in my traveling kit,
adolescent with longing
for everything laid out
before me, down on my knees
in the frigid air, on the first
night, asking for benevolence,
second chances without end.

Fay Chiang

Snow

snow falls in a hush under night lights, lampposts
doing waltzes.

I feel hopeful, though logic says to worry. we run
out of money with budget cuts in the arts, in
unemployment, food stamps, medicaid, housing. we've
got two hands apiece, we'll figure something out.

it snows now. tops of buildings covered white
and figures walking slowly past drifts on streets
below. pure spirits smokelike float on each snowflake
searching for kin.

put away the papers, stack the work for tomorrow,
turn the calendar page. each time the ritual
prepares for a new beginning. I walk slowly down
seven flights of darkened wooden stairs, past
other lofts filled with oiled machinery for small
industries. the front door opens and my coat is
caught by chill seeping through a hole in the
right pocket. shuddering I walk towards spring
street, past the iron security gates of the
carpenter, the chinese family coffee shop, the
rice and beans restaurant, the corner smoke shop.
people have gone home. they must be eating supper,
maybe watching t.v. or preparing a sandwich to
take to work, school. or maybe sick in bed with
this flu.

down spring street there are silent side streets,
loading bays scattered in snow, by workers

hurrying home at 5 p.m. windows reflect snow,
lamplight. they are eyes. I look past instead
staring skyward and search the darkness for
the source of this snow. but there are many
snowflakes and they swirl in patterns like
messengers, their secrets entwined in one
another, my figure swept up by their dances,
in motion.

I am excited: a warm glow in my chest expanding,
breathing. there is a song about living, about
being. I hear it when I walk through snow
under lamplight in city streets.

Edwin Rolfe

Season of Death

This is the sixth winter:
this is the season of death
when lungs contract and the breath of homeless men
freezes on restaurant window panes—men seeking
the sight of rare food
before the head is lowered into the upturned collar
and the shoulders hunched and the shuffling feet
move away slowly, slowly disappear
into a darkened street.

This is the season when rents go up:
men die, and their dying is casual.
I walk along a street, returning
at midnight from my unit. Meet a man
leaning against an illumined wall
and ask him for a light.
                                        His open eyes
stay fixed on mine. And cold rain falling
trickles down his nose, his chin.
"Buddy," I begin . . . and look more closely—
and flee in horror from the corpse's grin.

The eyes pursue you even in sleep and
when you awake they stare at you from the ceiling;
you see the dead face peering from your shoes;
the eggs at Thompson's are the dead man's eyes.
Work dims them for eight hours, but then—
the machines silent—they appear again.

Along the docks, in the terminals, in the subway, on the street,
in restaurants—the eyes

are focused from the river
among the floating garbage
that other men fish for,
their hands around poles
almost in prayer—
wanting to live,
wanting to live! who also soon
will stand propped by death against a stone-cold wall.

Sara Teasdale

From the Woolworth Tower

Vivid with love, eager for greater beauty
Out of the night we came
Into the corridor, brilliant and warm.
A metal door slides open,
And the lift receives us.
Swiftly, with sharp unswerving flight
The car shoots upward,
And the air, swirling and angry,
Howls like a hundred devils.
Past the maze of trim bronze doors,
Steadily we ascend
I cling to you
Conscious of the chasm under us,
And a terrible whirring deafens my ears.

The flight is ended.

We pass through a door leading onto the ledge—
Wind, night and space!
Oh terrible height
Why have we sought you?
Oh bitter wind with icy invisible wings
Why do you beat us?
Why would you bear us away?
We look through the miles of air,
The cold blue miles between us and the city,
Over the edge of eternity we look
On all the lights,
A thousand times more numerous than the stars;
Oh lines and loops of light in unwound chains

That mark for miles and miles
The vast black mazy cobweb of the streets;
Near us clusters and splashes of living gold
That change far off to bluish steel
Where the fragile lights on the Jersey shore
Tremble like drops of wind-stirred dew.
The strident noises of the city
Floating up to us
Are hallowed into whispers.
Ferries cross through the darkness
Weaving a golden thread into the night,
Their whistles weird shadows of sound.

We feel the millions of humanity beneath us,—
The warm millions, moving under the roofs,
Consumed by their own desires;
Preparing food,
Sobbing alone in a garret,
With burning eyes bending over a needle,
Aimlessly reading the evening paper,
Dancing in the naked light of the café,
Laying out the dead,
Bringing a child to birth—
The sorrow, the torpor, the bitterness, the frail joy
Come up to us
Like a cold fog wrapping us round,
Oh in a hundred years
Not one of these blood-warm bodies
But will be worthless as clay.
The anguish, the torpor, the toil
Will have passed to other millions
Consumed by the same desires.
Ages will come and go,
Darkness will blot the lights
And the tower will be laid on the earth.

The sea will remain
Black and unchanging,
The stars will look down
Brilliant and unconcerned.

Beloved,
Tho' sorrow, futility, defeat
Surround us,
They cannot bear us down.
Here on the abyss of eternity
Love has crowned us
For a moment
Victors.

ADRIENNE RICH

From Twenty-One Love Poems

XVI

Across a city from you, I'm with you,
just as an August night
moony, inlet-warm, seabathed, I watched you sleep,
the scrubbed, sheenless wood of the dressing-table
cluttered with our brushes, books, vials in the moonlight—
or a salt-mist orchard, lying at your side
watching red sunset through the screendoor of the cabin,
G minor Mozart on the tape-recorder,
falling asleep to the music of the sea.
This island of Manhattan is wide enough
for both of us, and narrow:
I can hear your breath tonight, I know how your face
lies upturned, the halflight tracing
your generous, delicate mouth
where grief and laughter sleep together.

XX

That conversation we were always on the edge
of having, runs on in my head,
at night the Hudson trembles in New Jersey light
polluted water yet reflecting even
sometimes the moon
and I discern a woman
I loved, drowning in secrets, fear wound round her throat
and choking her like hair. And this is she
with whom I tried to speak, whose hurt, expressive head
turning aside from pain, is dragged down deeper
where it cannot hear me,
and soon I shall know I was talking to my own soul.

Derek Walcott

God Rest Ye Merry, Gentlemen

Splitting from Jack Delaney's, Sheridan Square,
that winter night, stewed, seasoned in bourbon,
my body kindled by the whistling air
snowing the Village that Christ was reborn,
I lurched like any lush by his own glow
across towards Sixth, and froze before the tracks
of footprints bleeding on the virgin snow.
I tracked them where they led across the street
to the bright side, entering the wax-
sealed smell of neon, human heat,
some all-night diner with its wise-guy cook
his stub thumb in my bowl of stew and one
man's pulped and beaten face, its look
acknowledging all that, white-dark outside,
was possible: some beast prowling the block,
something fur-clotted, running wild
beyond the boundary of will. Outside,
more snow had fallen. My heart charred.
I longed for darkness, evil that was warm.
Walking, I'd stop and turn. What had I heard
wheezing behind my heel with whitening breath?
Nothing. Sixth Avenue yawned wet and wide.
The night was white. There was nowhere to hide.

Franz Wright

Arriving in the City

In the loose-fitting hospital gown,
holding a juglike container of blood
like a lantern,
the vein of a clear plastic tube running out of it
up one baggy sleeve,

disheveled and pale, you approached
down the aisle: on the night Greyhound
somewhere between New York City and Cleveland,
I abruptly woke up
with the distinct impression I'd screamed,

the one seated next to me still
fast asleep—I am walking
alone down Third Avenue now—those around me
all still fast asleep.

I find the address—it is on one
of those unlighted, unfrequented side streets
that are like passages
marked in a book
for undiscernible reasons.

The light is on.

I look up in the dark
faintly luminous blue hall of sky
between the walls
of locked warehouses.
Incontrovertibly,
the light is on.

I look up in the moon,
bathing the bones of my face in the cold
of that gray immaterial city
inhabited by eyeless millions, gazing
interminably at the world.

NATHANIEL PARKER WILLIS

City Lyrics

Argument.—The poet starts from the Bowling Green to take his sweetheart up to Thompson's for an ice, or (if she is inclined for more) ices. He confines his muse to matters which any every-day man and young woman may see in aking the same promenade for the same innocent refreshment.

Come out, love—the night is enchanting!
    The moon hangs just over Broadway;
The stars are all lighted and panting—
    (Hot weather up there, I dare say!)
'Tis seldom that "coolness" entices,
    And love is no better for chilling—
But come up to Thompson's for ices,
    And cool your warm heart for a shilling!

What perfume comes balmily o'er us?
    Mint juleps from City Hotel!
A loafer is smoking before us—
    (A nasty cigar, by the smell!)
Oh Woman! thou secret past knowing!
    Like lilachs that grow by the wall,
You breathe every air that is going,
    Yet gather but sweetness from all!

On, on! by St. Paul's, and the Astor!
    Religion seems very ill-plann'd!
For one day we list to the pastor,
    For six days we list to the band!
The sermon may dwell on the future,
    The organ your pulses may calm—
When—pest!—that remember'd cachucha
    Upsets both the sermon and psalm!

Oh, pity the love that must utter
    While goes a swift omnibus by!
(Though sweet is *I scream** when the flutter
    Of fans shows thermometers high)—
But if what I bawl, or I mutter,
    Falls into your ear but to die,
Oh, the dew that falls into the gutter
Is not more unhappy than I!

**Query.*—Should this be *Ice cream*, or I scream?—*Printer's Devil.*

Alberto O. Cappas

Maria's Journey

She was sitting there
The lonely traffic passing by
Thinking of yesterday when Mommy
Used to cry in protest
The warm air freezing her body
Listening to broken down voices of edited confusion
Subway rides traveling to nowhere
The wino on the corner learning to read
The New York Times
The polluted smell of everything hanging around her body
Thinking of yesterday when Fernando told her
"If you love me—you have to prove it"
She was sitting there
Hating the endless hours of the night
Those that passed looked at her with inviting eyes
That wanted to come out after her
Black and Puerto Rican kids playing Cowboys and Indians
After dark in the backyard streets
Where all of them
The Rats, the Dogs, the Cats, and the Pushers
Hold their daily meetings
She was sitting there
Hating herself for accepting a defeat that loved her
The lonely traffic passing by
Bars and liquor stores on every corner conditioning the
younger victims
While drug dealers count their money of death
Thinking of yesterday
Her trip from the island and her first introduction
To the New York cold that ravaged her body

Sitting there
Thinking of yesterday when Freddie played her wrong
Accusing her of being a puta for no reason at all
He is now happily married to a girl
From Queens who makes love to the Dog next door
Thinking of yesterday
The dances, the parties, and the James Bond movies
She loved so much
And now
Waiting for the overdose
Of everything to take effect.

Amy Lowell

New York at Night

A near horizon whose sharp jags
    Cut brutally into a sky
Of leaden heaviness, and crags
Of houses lift their masonry
    Ugly and foul, and chimneys lie
And snort, outlined against the gray
    Of lowhung cloud. I hear the sigh
The goaded city gives, not day
Nor night can ease her heart, her anguished labours stay.

Below, straight streets, monotonous,
    From north and south, from east and west,
Stretch glittering; and luminous
    Above, one tower tops the rest
    And holds aloft man's constant quest:
Time! Joyless emblem of the greed
    Of millions, robber of the best
Which earth can give, the vulgar creed
Has seared upon the night its flaming ruthless screed.

O Night! Whose soothing presence brings
    The quiet shining of the stars.
O Night! Whose cloak of darkness clings
    So intimately close that scars
    Are hid from our own eyes. Beggars
By day, our wealth is having night
    To burn our souls before altars
Dim and tree-shadowed, where the light
Is shed from a young moon, mysteriously bright.

Where art thou hiding, where thy peace?
        This is the hour, but thou art not.
Will waking tumult never cease?
        Hast thou thy votary forgot?
        Nature forsakes this man-begot
And festering wilderness, and now
        The long still hours are here, no jot
Of dear communing do I know;
Instead the glaring, man-filled city groans below!

Bob Dylan

From "Desolation Row"

They're selling postcards of the hanging
They're painting the passports brown
The beauty parlor is filled with sailors
The circus is in town
Here comes the blind commissioner
They've got him in a trance
One hand is tied to the tight-rope walker
The other is in his pants
And the riot squad they're restless
They need somewhere to go
As Lady and I look out tonight
From Desolation Row
. . .
Now the moon is almost hidden
The stars are beginning to hide
The fortune-telling lady
Has even taken all her things inside
All except for Cain and Abel
And the hunchback of Notre Dame
Everybody is making love
Or else expecting rain
And the Good Samaritan, he's dressing
He's getting ready for the show
He's going to the carnival tonight
On Desolation Row
. . .
Now at midnight all the agents
And the superhuman crew
Come out and round up everyone
That knows more than they do

Then they bring them to the factory
Where the heart-attack machine
Is strapped across their shoulders
And then the kerosene
Is brought down from the castles
By insurance men who go
Check to see that nobody is escaping
To Desolation Row
. . .

Léopold Sédar Senghor

To New York

(for jazz orchestra: trumpet solo)

I

New York! At first, I was confused by your beauty
    those big, long-legged golden girls.
So shy at first, before your blue metal eyes, your frosty smile
So very shy. And the anguish in the depth of the skyscraper streets
    owlish eyes raised in the eclipse of the sun.
Sulphurous your light and pale spires, whose tops
    strike into the sky,
Skyscrapers with muscles of steel and skins of burnished stone,
    defying tempests.
Fifteen days on the bare sidewalks of Manhattan
    —at the end of the third week the fever grips you
    with a jaguar's pounce—
Fifteen days and no well, no pasture, all the birds in flight
    drop dead just like that beneath the high ashen terraces
No laugh from a flowering child, his hand in my cool hand
No mother's breast, just nylon legs. Legs and breasts
    without sweat, without smell.
No tender words, no lips, nothing but artificial hearts
    paid for with hard cash.
And not a single book with wisdom. The painter's palette
    can only make coral crystals bloom.
Nights of insomnia, O nights of Manhattan! will-'o-the-wisps
    swirling, as horns blare the empty hours
As murky waters carry hygienic loves, like rivers bursting
    with children's corpses.

2

It is the time of signs and reckoning
New York! And yet, it is the time of manna and hyssop.
Just listen to God's trombones, to your
heart beating to the rhythm of blood your blood.
I saw in Harlem buzzing with sounds with ceremonial colors
with showy smells
—It's tea-time at the home of the pharmaceuticals
delivery-man—
I saw preparations for the Night festival at the retreat of day.
I proclaim Night more truthful than the day.
It is that pure hour, when God makes life from before memory
arise in the streets
And all the amphibious elements shine like suns.
Harlem Harlem! Here is what I saw Harlem Harlem!
A wind green with corn rise up from pavements
furrowed by the feet of Dans dansers
Hips silken waves, breasts iron spear, ballets
of waterlilies and fabulous masks
And mangoes of love rolling from low houses
upto the feet of police horses.
And all along the sidewalks I saw streams of white rum
streams of black milk in the blue fog of cigars.
At night I saw the sky snow down cotton flowers and angels'
wings and wizards' feathers.
Listen, New York! O listen to your male voice of brass
your vibrant oboe voice, anguish clogged with your tears
falling as great clots of blood
Listen to your nocturnal heart beating in the distance, rhythm
and blood of the tom-tom, tom-tom blood, tom-tom.

3

New York! New York I say, let black blood
flow in your blood
Let it clear rust from your steel joints, like an
oil of life

Let it give your bridges the curve of hips
        and the suppleness of vines.
It is the ancient times again, unity is rediscovered
        the Lion, the Bull and the Tree are reconciled.
Idea linked to act ear to heart sign to meaning.
See your rivers rustling with musk caimans and mirage-eyed
        manatees. No need to invent Sirens.
All you need do is open your eyes to the April rainbow
And your ears, especially your ears, to God, who with
        a saxophone's laugh created the heavens and the
        earth in six days.
And on the seventh day, he slept a deep Negro slumber.

—Translated from the French by Shawkat M. Toorawa

LANGSTON HUGHES

Juke Box Love Song

I could take the Harlem night
and wrap around you,
Take the neon lights and make a crown,
Take the Lenox Avenue busses,
Taxis, subways,
And for your love song tone their rumble down.
Take Harlem's heartbeat,
Make a drumbeat,
Put it on a record, let it whirl,
And while we listen to it play,
Dance with you till day—
Dance with you, my sweet brown Harlem girl.

Larry Fink, "Black Hand—Checkered Rump, N.Y.C.—May 1985," © Larry Fink 1991. Gelatin silver print. Herbert F. Johnson Museum of Art, Cornell University, Permanent Collection. Gift of Paula J. Mueller. Used by permission of the photographer.

ROBERT CLAIRMONT

These Ever Just So Six Million New York Hearts and Dorothy

Girl, you have breathed the scent of New York and now,
no greens, no flowers, no daisies . . . not even the wind on greens and flowers can hold you long.
You will not stay on prairie wastes, girl, for you have listened to the rivers of Manhattan at nighttime: you have been quite too near these ever just so six million New York hearts: you have watched quite too many New York sunsets and dawns.
You'll come back, girl: quite soon these ever just so New York floors and stones will feel your quick, sharp walk.
You cannot stay with prairie wastes and flowers, girl, for you have breathed the scent of New York too long.
You have been quite too near these ever just so six million New York hearts; and they will someday call you back, girl.

Further Reading

(Listed chronologically)

The Open Door: One Hundred Poems, One Hundred Years of Poetry *Magazine*, edited by Don Share and Christian Wiman. Chicago and London: University of Chicago Press, 2012.

Good Poems, American Places, selected and introduced by Garrison Keillor. New York: Viking, 2011.

Writing New York: A Literary Anthology, expanded edition, edited by Phillip Lopate. New York: Library of America, 2008.

I Speak of the City: Poems of New York, selected and edited by Stephen Wolf, foreword by John Hollander. New York: Columbia University Press, 2007.

Broken Land: Poems of Brooklyn, edited by Julia Spicher Kasdorf and Michael Tyrell, foreword by Hal Sirowitz. New York: New York University Press, 2007.

New York Poets II: An Anthology: From Edwin Denby to Bernadette Mayer, edited by Mark Ford and Trevor Winkfield. Manchester: Carcanet, 2006.

The New York Poets: Frank O'Hara, John Ashbery, Kenneth Koch, James Schuyler: An Anthology, edited with an introduction by Mark Ford. Manchester: Carcanet, 2004.

Poetry After 9-11: An Anthology of New York Poets, edited by Dennis Loy Johnson, introduction by Alicia Ostriker. Hoboken: Melville House, 2002.

Poems of New York, selected and edited by Elizabeth Schmidt. New York: Alfred A. Knopf, 2002.

New York: Poems, edited by Howard Moss. New York: Avon, 1980.

An Anthology of New York Poets, edited by Ron Padgett and David Shapiro, drawings by Joe Brainard. New York: Random House, 1970.

Biographical Details

Poets

Adonis (b. 'Ali Ahmad Sa'id in Latakia, Syria, 1930) is an Arab poet, critic, translator and artist. *Adonis: Selected Poems* (2010), translated by Khaled Mattawa, received a PEN Award for Literary Translation. In 2011, Adonis was awarded the Goethe Prize.

Maya Angelou (b. St. Louis, Missouri, 1928; d. Winston-Salem, North Carolina, 2014) was nominated for the Pulitzer Prize for her first collection, *Just Give Me a Cool Drink of Water 'Fore I Diiie* (1971). She has received three Grammys for spoken word albums and in 2000 received the National Medal of Arts.

W. H. Auden (b. York, England, 1907; d. Vienna, Austria, 1973) moved to the United States in 1939. He won a National Book Award for Poetry for *The Shield of Achilles* in 1956 and in 1967 received the National Medal for Literature. His *Collected Poems* appeared in 1991.

Gwendolyn Bennett (b. Gidding, Texas, 1902; d. Reading, Pennsylvania, 1981) was active in the Harlem Renaissance, notably as an organizer of a writers' support group. Her poems appeared principally in the journal *Opportunity*, published by the National Urban League.

Ted Berrigan (b. Providence, Rhode Island, 1934; d. New York City, 1983) was active in Chicago and then as a member of the second generation of New York School poets. *The Sonnets* appeared in 1964 and his *Collected Poems* posthumously in 2005.

ANNA HEMPSTEAD BRANCH (1875–1937, New London, Connecticut) was a poet and social worker associated with Christodora House, a social settlement in New York City's Lower East Side. *Sonnets from a Lock Box* appeared in 1929 and the posthumous *Last Poems* in 1944.

LUIS CABALQUINTO (b. Magarao, Philippines, 1935) came to the United States in 1968. His poetry, in English and in two Filipino languages, is widely anthologized. His most recent book of poems is *Mannahatta Mahal* (2007).

ALBERTO O. CAPPAS (b. Yauco, Puerto Rico, 1946) has published three volumes of poetry, the most recent of which is *Doña Julia* (2009). In 2007, he founded the Educational Pledge Partnership and has been its president since. Cappas lives in New York City.

FAY CHIANG (b. New York City, 1952) founded the Basement Workshop in the Lower East Side, as well as Project Reach. Her first collection, *In the City of Contradictions*, appeared in 1979. She has edited several anthologies and is currently working on a book-length poem.

ROBERT CLAIRMONT (b. Pittsburgh, Pennsylvania, 1902), a prominent figure in Greenwich Village, was the founder of *New Cow of Greenwich Village* and the editor of *Pegasus* in the 1950s. His poetry collections include *Quintillions* (1928) and *Forever X* (1951).

HART CRANE (b. 1899, d. Gulf of Mexico, 1932) moved to New York City in 1916. His first collection, *White Buildings*, appeared in 1926, and his long poem, *The Bridge*, appeared in 1930. *Collected Poems* appeared posthumously in 1938 and *The Complete Poems* in 1986.

VICTOR HERNÁNDEZ CRUZ (b. Aguas Buenas, Puerto Rico, 1949) is a Nuyorican poet who now divides his time between Morocco and Puerto Rico. *In the Shadow of al-Andalus* appeared in 2011. *Maraca: New and Selected Poems, 1965–2000* (2001) was shortlisted for the Griffin Prize.

E. E. CUMMINGS (b. Cambridge, Massachusetts, 1894; d. North Conway, New Hampshire, 1962) was an essayist, playwright, and poet who frequently experimented with form. His *Collected Poems* appeared in 1960. His many awards include the 1958 Bollingen Prize.

MAHMOUD DARWISH (b. al-Birwa, British Mandate of Palestine, 1941; d. Houston, Texas, 2008) was an Arabic poet and the de facto poet laureate of Palestine. In 2004, he received the Prince Claus Award. *The Butterfly's Burden* (translated by Fady Joudah) appeared in 2007.

BOB DYLAN (b. Duluth, Minnesota, 1941) has received eleven Grammys for his music and lyrics, was inducted into the Songwriters Hall of Fame in 1982, and in 2008 received both a Pulitzer Prize Special Citation and the National Medal of Arts. His latest album is *Tempest* (2012).

SHOKRY ELDALY (b. New York City, 1986) is a 2011 Pushcart Prize nominee and recipient of the Blanche Colton Williams Fellowship. His poetry has appeared in several journals, including the *Sixers Review*. He is presently at work on a novel.

MARTÍN ESPADA (b. New York City, 1957) has published seventeen books as a poet, essayist, editor, and translator. *The Republic of Poetry* (2006) was a Pulitzer Prize finalist in 2007. His most recent collection is *The Trouble Ball* (2012).

ALLEN GINSBERG (b. Newark, New Jersey, 1926; d. New York City, 1997) was a prominent poet of the 1950's Beat Generation. *The*

Fall of America (1973) shared the National Book Award for Poetry. The long poem *Howl* (1956) is Ginsberg's best-known work.

Nikki Giovanni (b. Knoxville, Tennessee, 1943) is an activist, children's author, and poet. *The Collected Poetry of Nikki Giovanni, 1968–1998* appeared in 2003, and *The Nikki Giovanni Poetry Collection* was nominated for a 2004 Grammy Award for Best Spoken Word Album.

Durs Grünbein (b. Dresden, East Germany, 1962) is one of Germany's most important poets. In 1995, he received the Georg-Büchner-Preis. In 2006, *Ashes for Breakfast: Selected Poems* (translated by Michael Hoffman) was shortlisted for the International Griffin Poetry Prize.

Jessica Hagedorn (b. Manila, Philippines, 1949) moved to San Francisco in 1963, then to New York City in 1978. She is a playwright, novelist, multimedia artist, anthologist, and poet. Her novel *Dogeaters* was nominated for a 1990 National Book Award.

John Hollander (b. New York City, 1929; d. Branford, Connecticut) wrote two dozen poetry collections. In 1958, W. H. Auden selected his *A Crackling of Thorns* for the Yale Younger Poets Series. He received the Bollingen Prize in 1983 and a MacArthur Fellowship in 1990.

Langston Hughes (b. Joplin, Missouri, 1902; d. New York City, 1967) was a poet, novelist, playwright, and children's author active during the Harlem Renaissance. He was made a member of the National Institute of Arts and Letters in 1961. *The Collected Poems* appeared in 1994.

Donald Justice (b. Miami, Florida, 1925; d. Iowa City, Iowa, 2004) received the Pulitzer Prize for *Selected Poems* (1979), the Bollingen Prize in 1991, and a National Book Award for *Collected Poems* (2004).

Galway Kinnell (b. Providence, Rhode Island, 1927) won the Pulitzer Prize and the National Book Award in 1982 for *Selected Poems*. From 1989 to 1993 he was Poet Laureate of Vermont. He has translated Yves Bonnefoy, François Villon, and Rainer Marie Rilke.

Stephanie Krueger (b. Sioux Falls, South Dakota, 1971) has published poems in *Spirit of Bosnia* and *Diwan*. Krueger became a New York City resident in 2005 and since then has been living in SoHo, West Harlem, and Astoria.

Denise Levertov (b. Ilford, England, 1923; d. Seattle, Washington, 1997) moved to New York City in 1948. She wrote twenty books of poetry and criticism, for which she received several awards, including the Robert Frost Medal of the Poetry Society of America.

Vachel Lindsay (1879–1931, Springfield, Illinois) was known as the "Prairie Troubadour" for his views on singing poetry, detailed in his correspondence with Yeats. *Poetry* magazine awarded him a lifetime achievement award in 1928. His *Complete Poetry* was published in 1984.

Federico García Lorca (b. Fuente Vaqueros, Spain, 1898; d. Fuente Grande, Spain, 1936) came to New York City in 1929. *Poet in New York* was published posthumously in 1942; a new critical edition appeared in 2012.

Amy Lowell (1874–1925, Brookline, Massachusetts) won the Pulitzer Prize posthumously in 1926 for *What's O'Clock*. *The Complete Poetical Works of Amy Lowell* appeared in 1925. It was published again with some missing material in 1955.

Robert Lowell (b. Boston, Massachusetts, 1917; d. New York City, 1977) won the Pulitzer Prize in 1947 for *Lord Weary's Castle* and in 1974 for *The Dolphin*. His *Collected Poems* appeared in 2003.

Anna Margolin (b. Brest, Belarus, 1887; d. 1952, New York City) was the pen name of the Yiddish poet Rosa Harning Lebensboym. She traveled to New York City in 1906 and settled there in 1913. In 1929, she published *Poems*, her one volume of poetry.

Kenneth McClane (b. 1951, New York City) is a poet and essayist. His most recent book, *Color: Essays on Race, Family, and History*, won the 2009 Book of the Year Award for Essays from *ForeWord* magazine.

Claude McKay (b. Nairne Castle, Jamaica, 1889; d. Chicago, Illinois, 1948) moved to New York City in 1914, left for Europe in 1919, and returned in 1921. His *Harlem Shadows* (1922) was an early product of the Harlem Renaissance. His *Complete Poems* appeared in 2003.

Edna St. Vincent Millay (b. Rockland, Maine, 1892; d. Austerlitz, New York, 1950) moved to New York City in 1917. *The Ballad of the Harp-Weaver* won the 1923 Pulitzer Prize. In 1943, she was awarded the Robert Frost Medal of the Poetry Society of America.

Valzhyna Mort (b. Minsk, Belarus, 1981) moved to the United States in 2005. Her *Factory of Tears* (2008) was the first bilingual Belarusian-English poetry collection published in the United States. In 2010, she received the Bess Hokin Prize from *Poetry* magazine. *Collected Body* appeared in 2011.

Frank O'Hara (b. Baltimore, Maryland, 1926; d. Fire Island, New York, 1966) was a member of the New York School. Lawrence Ferlinghetti commissioned *Lunch Poems* (1964) for City Lights. His posthumous *Collected Poems* shared the National Book Award in 1972.

Sharon Olds (b. San Francisco, California, 1942) received the National Book Critics Circle Award in 1984 for *The Dead and*

Living. From 1998 to 2000 she was New York State Poet Laureate. In 2012, she became the first American to win the T. S. Eliot Prize, for *Stag's Leap*.

NICANOR PARRA (b. San Fabián de Alico, Chile, 1914) received Chile's National Literature Award in 1969 and again in 1981. In 2011, he won the Cervantes Prize. *After-Dinner Declarations* (translated by Dave Oliphant) appeared in a bilingual edition in 2009.

WILLIE PERDOMO (b. 1967, New York City) is a poet and children's author. He received the New York Foundation for the Arts Award in 2001, and *Smoking Lovely* (2003) received a PEN Beyond Margins Award. He is founder and codirector of Cypher Books.

MELANIE REHAK (b. New York City, 1971) is a journalist, writer, poet, and critic. While on fellowship at New York Public Library's Cullman Center for Scholars and Writers, she wrote the Edgar Award-winning novel *Girl Sleuth*.

ADRIENNE RICH (b. Baltimore, Maryland, 1929; d. Santa Cruz, California, 2012) received numerous awards for her poetry, including a National Book Award for *Diving into the Wreck* (1974), the inaugural Ruth Lilly Poetry Prize in 1986, and a MacArthur Fellowship in 1994.

EDWIN ROLFE (b. Philadelphia, Pennsylvania, 1909; d. Hollywood, California, 1954) published *To My Contemporaries* in New York City in 1936. His last collection, *Permit Me* (1955), appeared posthumously. His *Collected Poems* appeared in 1993.

CARL SANDBURG (b. Galesburg, Illinois, 1878; d. Flat Rock, North Carolina, 1967) received the Pulitzer Prize for *Corn Huskers* (1919) and *The Complete Poems* (1951). In 1959 he received a Grammy for his recording of Copland's "Lincoln Portrait" with the New York Philharmonic.

James Schuyler (b. Chicago, Illinois, 1923; d. New York City, 1991) moved to New York City in the late 1940s where he was part of the New York School of poets. He received the Pulitzer Prize for his 1980 collection, *The Morning of the Poem.*

David Semanki (b. Connecticut, 1971) has published in *The New Yorker*, *American Poetry Review*, *The Yale Review*, and *The Paris Review*. He edited and wrote the commentary for Sylvia Plath's *Ariel: The Restored Edition* (2004).

Léopold Sédar Senghor (b. Joal, French West Africa [Senegal], 1906; d. Verson, France, 2001) was a poet, theorist, and President of Senegal from 1960 to 1980. His *Collected Poetry* (translated by Melvin Dixon) appeared in English in 1991.

Purvi Shah (b. Ahmedabad, India, 1972) was a poetry editor for the *Asian Pacific American Journal* and is now a consultant on violence against women, and language and media issues in New York City. *Terrain Tracks* (2006) won the Many Voices Project competition.

Meredith Shepard (b. Berkeley, California, 1987) studied literature and human rights at Cornell University, where she wrote "Why I Hate New York." She is writing a memoir about working in Rwanda.

Charles Simic (b. Belgrade, Yugoslavia, 1938) received the Pulitzer Prize in 1990 for *The World Doesn't End* and the Griffin Poetry Prize in 2004 for *Selected Poems, 1963–2003*. He was a MacArthur Fellow from 1984 to 1989 and U.S. Poet Laureate in 2007–2008.

Paul Simon (b. Newark, New Jersey, 1941) has won twelve Grammys for his music and lyrics and in 2007 was the first recipient of the Library of Congress Gershwin Award for Popular Music. In 2011, he was inducted into the American Academy of Arts and Sciences.

SASHA SKENDERIJA (b. Vitez, Bosnia, former Yugoslavia, 1968) divides his time between Ithaca, New York, and Prague. He writes principally in Bosnian. English translations of his work include *Why the Dwarf Had to Be Shot* (2008) and *Cape of Good Hope* (2011).

TOM SLEIGH (b. Mount Pleasant, Texas, 1953) received a Shelley Memorial Award in 1999, an award from the American Academy of Arts and Letters in 2003, and the 2008 Kingsley Tufts Award for *Space Walk*. Sleigh lives in Brooklyn, New York.

HERMAN SPECTOR (1905–1959, New York City) was associated with the magazines *Dynamo* and *Blues* in the late 1920s and early 1930s. *Bastard in the Ragged Suit: Writings of, with Drawings by, Herman Spector* appeared in 1977.

SARA TEASDALE (b. Saint Louis, Missouri, 1884; d. New York City, 1933) moved to New York City in 1916 and in 1918 won the Pulitzer Prize and the annual award of the Poetry Society of America for *Love Songs* (1917).

TOMAS TRANSTRÖMER (b. Stockholm, Sweden, 1931) has been translated into sixty languages. In 1990, he received the Neustadt International Prize for Literature and in 2011 the Nobel Prize in Literature. An updated *Collected Poems* appeared in 2011.

DEREK WALCOTT (b. Castries, Saint Lucia, 1930) published *In a Green Night: Poems 1948–1960* in 1962. His epic poem, *Omeros*, appeared in 1990 and in 1992 he received the Nobel Prize in Literature. *White Egrets* (2010) received the T. S. Eliot Prize.

WALT WHITMAN (b. West Hills, New York, 1819; d. Camden, New Jersey, 1892) was a poet, journalist, government clerk, and volunteer nurse during the American Civil War. He continuously revised *Leaves of Grass*, which first appeared in 1855.

Anne Pierson Wiese (b. Minneapolis, Minnesota, 1964) is author of *Floating City* (2007), chosen by Kay Ryan for the Academy of American Poets Walt Whitman Award. Her work has appeared in *Ploughshares*, *The Hudson Review*, *The Southern Review*, *Raritan*, and elsewhere.

Nathaniel Parker Willis (b. Portland, Maine, 1806; d. Cambridge, Massachusetts, 1867) was a poet, playwright, and journalist whose popularity declined in his later years. As editor of the *Home Journal*, he promoted the work of women poets.

Franz Wright (b. Vienna, Austria, 1953) won the 2004 Pulitzer Prize for *Walking to Martha's Vineyard*. His most recent collection is *Kindertotenwald: Prose Poems* (2011). He is also an accomplished translator.

Translators

Munir Akash teaches at Suffolk University. His collaborative translations of Mahmoud Darwish include *Unfortunately, It Was Paradise* (2003) with Carolyn Forché and *State of Siege* (2010) with Daniel Abdal-Hayy Moore.

E. Wayles Browne teaches languages and linguistics at Cornell University, is an editor of Slavic journals in several countries, and translates widely from Slavic languages. He has been Sasha Skenderija's principal translator since 1993.

Carolyn Forché is an award-winning poet, anthologist, and translator, and also a teacher, activist, and human rights advocate. She has translated the poetry of Mahmoud Darwish (with Munir Akash), Claribel Alegría, and Robert Desnos (with William Kulick).

Robin Fulton is a Scottish poet and translator who spent most of his adult life as a university lecturer in Norway. He has translated many Scandinavian poets, including Kjell Espmark, Olav Hauge, Harry Martinson, and Tomas Tranströmer.

SHIRLEY KUMOVE has published two bilingual collections of Yiddish folk sayings, and edited and translated the collected poems of Anna Margolin in *Drunk for the Bitter Truth* (2005).

ANDREW SHIELDS teaches English language and literature at the University of Basel. He is a poet, translator, songwriter, and guitarist. He has translated, among numerous others, Ilma Rakusa from German and Jacques Réda from French.

SHAWKAT M. TOORAWA translates from Arabic, French, Mauritian Creole, and Spanish. His translation of Adonis, *A Time Between Ashes and Roses: Poems*, appeared in 2004. He is an executive editor of the Library of Arabic Literature, a series of editions/translations.

LIZ WERNER is a poet, novelist, and essayist who translates between English and Spanish. She has lived and worked in Chile and has translated Jimmy Santiago Baca and Nicanor Parra.

ELIZABETH OEHLKERS WRIGHT translates contemporary German poets, including the German-Turkish Zafer Şenocak and Zehra Çirak. With her husband, Franz Wright, she has translated Valzhyna Mort's *Factory of Tears* (2008) from Belarusian.

FRANZ WRIGHT, a Pulitzer Prize–winning poet, has translated René Char from French, Rainer Maria Rilke from German, and, with his wife, Elizabeth Oehlkers Wright, Valzhyna Mort from Belarusian.

Chronology of Poems

1844	"City Lyrics," by Nathaniel Parker Willis
1860, 1867	"When I Heard at the Close of the Day," by Walt Whitman
1905	"New York at Sunrise," by Anna Hempstead Branch
1906	"Broadway," by Carl Sandburg
1912	"New York at Night," by Amy Lowell
1914	"A Rhyme about an Electrical Advertising Sign," by Vachel Lindsay
1915	"From the Woolworth Tower," by Sara Teasdale
1922	"Dawn in New York," by Claude McKay
	"MacDougal Street," by Edna St. Vincent Millay
1924	"at the ferocious phenomenon," by E. E. Cummings
1925	"These Ever Just So Six Million New York Hearts and Dorothy," by Robert Clairmont
1926	"Street Lamps in Early Spring," by Gwendolyn Bennett
1927	"To Brooklyn Bridge," by Hart Crane
1929	"Evening on Fifth Avenue," by Anna Margolin

1931	"New York (Office and Denunciation)," by Federico García Lorca
1935	"Season of Death," by Edwin Rolfe
1939	"Wiseguy Type," by Herman Spector
	"September 1, 1939," by W. H. Auden
1950	"Juke Box Love Song," by Langston Hughes
1956	"A Step Away from Them," by Frank O'Hara
	"To New York," by Léopold Sédar Senghor
1957	"February Evening in New York," by Denise Levertov
1960	"The Avenue Bearing the Initial of Christ into the New World," by Galway Kinnell
1964	"Sonnet XXXVI," by Ted Berrigan
1965	"Desolation Row," by Bob Dylan
	"God Rest Ye Merry, Gentlemen," by Derek Walcott
1966	"The 59th Street Bridge Song (Feelin' Groovy)," by Paul Simon
1967	"Central Park," by Robert Lowell
1970	"New York," by John Hollander
1971	"A Grave for New York," by Adonis
1974	"Mugging," by Allen Ginsberg
	"Twenty-One Love Poems," by Adrienne Rich
1975	"As Fate Would Have It," by Mahmoud Darwish
	"Latin Music in New York," by Jessica Hagedorn

1978	"The New Yorkers," by Nikki Giovanni
	"Schubertiana," by Tomas Tranströmer
1981	"Sunday Morning," by Kenneth McClane
1982	"Snow," by Fay Chiang
	"Arriving in the City," by Franz Wright
1983	"Awaking in New York," by Maya Angelou
1984	"Manhattan Dawn (1945)," by Donald Justice
	"The morning," by James Schuyler
1985	"Resurrection," by Nicanor Parra
1987	"Summer Solstice, New York City," by Sharon Olds
1992	"Early Morning in July," by Charles Simic
1996	"123rd Street Rap," by Willie Perdomo
1997	"The Lower East Side of Manhattan," by Victor Hernández Cruz
2000	"The Mexican Cabdriver's Poem for His Wife, Who Has Left Him," by Martín Espada
2001	"August Walk," by Luis Cabalquinto
2002	"Maria's Journey," by Alberto O. Cappas
	"New York American Spell, 2001," by Tom Sleigh
2006	"Made in India, Immigrant Song #3," by Purvi Shah
	"Autobiography: New York," by Melanie Rehak
2007	"New York," by Valzhyna Mort
	"Body Elite," by Anne Pierson Wiese

2009	"Cyclone," by Stephanie Krueger
2010	"Why I Hate New York," by Meredith Shepard
	"I Had This Dream/the city of shadows," by Shokry Eldaly
	"Rain," by David Semanki
2011	"West Side Story," by Sasha Skenderija
	"Peacocks on Broadway," by Durs Grünbein

*Note that, in some cases, the date perforce reflects year of publication rather than year of composition.

Index of First Lines

Index of Titles

Index of Poets